HAUNTED CANADIAN COUNTY

HAUNTED CANADIAN COUNTY

TANYA MCCOY & WHITNEY WILSON

Haunted America

Published by Haunted America
A Division of The History Press
Charleston, SC
www.historypress.com

First published 2018

Opposite: Billy Jack Reuter. *Courtesy of Vicki Proctor*.

Manufactured in the United States

ISBN 9781467141543

Library of Congress Control Number: 2018945676

In Memory of
Billy Jack Reuter

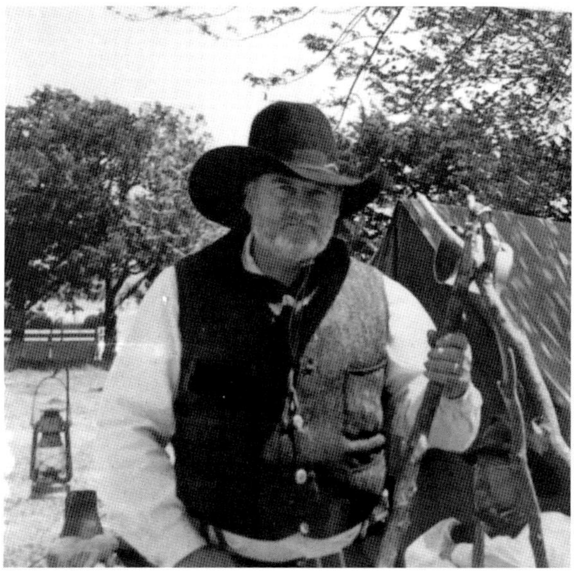

A true cowboy, who helped to preserve the history of Canadian County. He and his wife, Pat Reuter, collected and preserved vital pieces of Oklahoma history and formed the Canadian County Historical Museum in El Reno, Oklahoma, as well as donated many other artifacts to various other museums to share with us and many generations to come. Thank you, Mr. Reuter, for helping to keep history alive for all of us.

To my youngest daughter, Katy McCoy,
for all the time away while writing this book.—Tanya

For my husband, Josh; and kids, Dane and Lyric,
for tolerating me and my time away.—Whitney

CONTENTS

Contents

Acknowledgements

A special thanks to the Cheyenne-Arapaho Nation; Max Bear, Calvin White of Just Paranormal Stuff; the Canadian County Historical Museum; Pat Reuter; Vicki Proctor; Judy Mihn; the Oklahoma Historical Society; the Mustang Historical Society; Carole Hanna; the Elks Lodge of El Reno; Cortney Kane Sites; Jennifer Handley; the City of El Reno; Heather Brothers; the National Cavalry Museum; Wendy Ogden; the Fort Reno Historical Society; Jim Johnston; Ron Cross, founder of PROS (Paranormal Research of Organized Studies) Investigations; Kale Epperson and Jeri Beavers of Paranormal Investigations of Oklahoma; the City of Mustang; Gayle Early; our OPA (Oklahoma Paranormal Association) teammates and besties Cara Pershall and Dana Rutledge; several contributors who wish to be left unnamed; and, of course, our wonderful supportive husbands, Joshua Wilson and Clinton Womack-McCoy.

INTRODUCTION

INTRODUCTION TO PARANORMAL INVESTIGATION

Through the centuries, people from across the world have shared their ghostly encounters. When you become involved with ghost hunting or, as we like to call it, paranormal investigating, you must first understand what a spirit or haunting truly is. Reaching the paranormal has become more popular and widely more accepted over the past decade due to the recent rise in paranormal shows on television. Even though most of the shows are over dramatized and some even faked for ratings, the fact is that paranormal activity does occur. Just keep in mind that not everything that happens is paranormal. When investigating, it is best to use a scientific view and see if you can find a reason why such things might be occurring. For instance, is the knocking sound you are hearing coming from a loose window screen or a tree limb hitting the house? Did the door that just slowly open have a weak catch that is easily moved or has the house settled, causing it to pitch and make the floor uneven? Often a strange image in a picture can be caused by a light flare or reflection. Please keep in mind that dust particles captured on film do not constitute an orb. It is also necessary to do your research prior to ever investigating, not only on the location but in the paranormal field as well. It's hard to conduct a proper investigation if you don't know what you're doing or even what you are dealing with.

There are several different types of hauntings, as well as different terms being used in the field of paranormal research. What equipment you may choose to use will depend on the location and what type of haunting it is. To help you better understand some of our experiences, we will first discuss the type of hauntings written about in this book and some of the equipment we often use.

What is a ghost or spirit? The study of the paranormal is still in its early stages, even though it has been in research for the past two centuries. Most of what we know, or think we know, is based on theory and personal experiences. Much like the study of medicine, it will take us more time to possibly be able to explain and prove or disprove the existence of a ghost. The present theory behind the existence of a ghost is that it is a person who has passed on, leaving their earthly body behind while their spirit moves on to another plane of existence. Scientists have proven that each one of our cells contains a small battery pack called ATP (adenosine triphosphate), which is a molecule in the nucleotide. The molecule is able to store and transmit energy within the cell. The question is, when our body dies, where does that energy go? Many people believe that it is that energy that is our actual soul, and that the soul leaves the body, which causes the body to die. For years, when someone would pass, a family member or even nurses I have worked with in the past have opened a window so the spirit would have a way to leave. Many cultures still cover all the mirrors in the house so the spirit won't become trapped in their glass. Is it possible that certain spirits don't cross over to the other realm, and that's why so many people are claiming to see ghostly apparitions to this day? To better understand a haunting, we must figure out what type of haunting it actually is.

One type of haunting we often encounter is called an intelligent haunting, which is when you come in contact with a spirit that can interact with you. For example, if a spirit responds to the knock test—a test where you knock a certain number of times or use a special rhythm and then ask the spirit to repeat it for you—then it is considered an intelligent haunting. These types of spirits are also known to interact by moving objects, turning on lights or setting off sensors on command.

A photographic haunting, or residual haunting, is just the opposite of an intelligent haunting. It never interacts, and it plays over and over like a scene from a movie. For example, if you witnessed a woman in a long blue dress walking up the stairs during a certain type of day or night but she never turned to acknowledge you or interact but is always seen doing the same activity, then she is a photographic haunting. Photographic hauntings are believed to be caused by a large burst of energy caused during a person's life where they leave an ever-lasting imprint on time, much like a photograph or movie. A person's feelings can send out a large charge of energy, often marking the area with what appears to be an imprint on time.

A poltergeist haunting, also known as a noisy ghost, may or may not be an actual spirit. I do believe that spirits can manipulate the atmosphere and move objects by using a large amount of energy and force, but I also believe that some people do have the power of telekinesis without even realizing it. After all, science has proven that we only use a small percentage of our brains' capability, and some people use even less. These cases are most often found when a young teenager is involved. It is believed that when teenagers are going through life changes, their emotions and energy are out of whack, causing an energy shift that can, in turn, move objects. If there is a poltergeist haunting being caused by an actual spirit, then it is more likely haunting that particular person and not the location. That being said, some intelligent hauntings can produce poltergeist activity as well.

A demonic haunting is exactly what it sounds like: a demonic. A demon is something that has never been human. The word *demonic* originates from the Latin word *daemonicus*, referring to a supernatural being with superhuman powers. It is considered to be a spirit intermediate between God and humans associated with Lucifer, better known as Satan, an outcast angel from heaven. Reports of demonic possession have occurred for centuries, and it has been claimed that some people have even died from demonic possession. Over the years, I have met several paranormal teams that claim to have come across demonic cases. Even though we have seen a rise in cases, most people jump to calling a haunting demonic prior to learning all the facts. A demonic haunting is a rarity and often is nothing more than just an angry spirit or one trying to make someone believe it is more powerful than it truly is.

To try to determine if a haunting truly exists and what type of haunting it may be, we use several different pieces of equipment. Cameras—both still frame as well as night-vision video cameras—are always essential for gathering possible paranormal activity. The downfall to using a camera is the capturing of orbs. Orbs are bright balls of light often seen flying through the air. They can take on different colors, but they can also be mislabeled by paranormal researchers or enthusiasts. Many different things can cause an orb effect on camera; usually it's dust particles in the air, but they can also be caused by moisture, bugs and even cobwebs. Another known abnormality that can occur on film is called a rod. It's often produced by cameras capturing an elongated artifact of something moving quickly in the air. It is often associated with cryptozoologists and ufologists in the study of UFOs, but some paranormal researchers associate it with a possible spirit flying through the area. An SLS camera can also be used to determine shadow movement using a Kinect software, found in your common Wii video games, to form a stick outline to show movements of someone or something walking through a space.

Voice recorders are always used in hopes of gathering an EVP, or electronic voice phenomenon. It is believed that a voice recorder can pick up sound waves on various levels, making it possible for spirits to communicate with us. I still remember the time I captured my first EVP. There are three types of EVPs: Classes A, B and C. Class A is an EVP that is so clear that you can tell exactly what is being said. Class B is a recording where you can make out bits and pieces of what the spirit is saying, and Class C is where you can hear that something is being said but you can't hear it clearly enough to make out what it is saying.

Another popular piece of equipment we use are EMF (electromagnetic field) detectors. There are a few different versions of the EMF detector. The K2 and ghost meter, also known as an electromagnetic detector, detect electromagnetic energy in the area. The theory behind using this device is that spirits leave behind an energy field in the area they may be in or may have been in. It is also used as a piece of equipment to interact with spirits by having them manipulate the device to light it up or make it sound. Unfortunately, this device can also pick up on nonparanormal activity such as energy caused by cellphones, lights, electrical equipment, police radios, CB radios or walkie-talkies, often giving off false readings. It's best to always use two different types of equipment to help substantiate any possible activity that might occur.

The FLIR (forward-looking infrared) camera detects infrared energy (heat) and converts it into an electronic signal. It then takes that signal and produces a thermal image on a monitor or screen, often showing the outline of an object or spirit. It also helps to outline cold spots. It is theorized that spirits will use the energy in the air to help manifest, leaving behind a cold spot.

The Parascope, created by Jeromy Jones of Paranologies, is a device used to detect an energy level produced by a static electricity type of event. Clear rod-like structures protrude out from the base, which lights up in different rainbow colors to help determine from which direction the energy field is being produced. We have also experienced spirits being able to manipulate the energy field to light up a certain number of rods on demand.

A ghost box is a radio rewired to scan radio stations nonstop. The theory behind this device is that spirits can manipulate the energy waves and stations to help produce words to better communicate with us. Personally, the constant static noise drives me insane, so I prefer Ghost Radio. Ghost Radio is an application you can find on most phones. Most ghost-hunting applications you download from the phone do not work, but we have used this particular application for many years and have had some very good results from it. Ghost Radio, created by Exelerus, detects different energy levels in the air, and each level is attached to a large word bank. The theory behind this application is that the spirit can manipulate the energy levels to be able to communicate with us. There is another piece of equipment on the market that uses the same type of programming but why pay more for it when you can have the same—or in our case better—results for 1/1000 of the price?

Paranormal investigating isn't cheap and equipment can become very expensive, but there some cheaper pieces of equipment that you can use to start out in the field. A compass is good to use to detect a shift in the energy field. Dowsing rods can also be used to find an energy field. A small mag flashlight, a touch sensor light or a motion sensor light can be used to help spirits communicate with the dimming of the light. A temperature gun can be found for under thirty dollars at most home improvement shops and will help detect cold spots. With all the different pieces of equipment out there on the market, never forget that the best piece of equipment is you. Our own senses tell us when things don't seem quite right—the chills you feel on your arm or the back of your neck or perhaps that feeling of being watched. People often refer to me as a psychic or medium, but I always tell them I am no different from anyone else. Everyone has the ability to see or feel things; we are born with it. Whether it be a sixth sense or a mother's intuition, it is like any other muscle in your body: the more you use it, the stronger it will become; the less you use it, the weaker it becomes. What it comes down to at the end of the day is what you wish to do with it.

Please keep in mind that if you choose to do paranormal research, study the field first and never trespass. As a paranormal investigator, one of my main rules is to never provoke, and that is what we like to teach people. We believe in not provoking for a couple of reasons. First, would you walk into someone's home and start cursing at them and demanding they show themselves? You don't know who you are talking to. It could be a spirit of an elderly grandmother or a young child who doesn't understand why they are there. Second, you could make the spirit very angry, and some do have the ability to hurt you or follow you home. It's always best to be respectful and careful when it comes to the spirit world because you never know exactly what you will find there.

Introduction to Canadian County

Canadian County is located just west of Oklahoma City and consists of 905.17 square miles of land and water. Named after the Canadian River that runs through it, this area played a critical part in developing the state of Oklahoma. Originally part of the Louisiana Purchase, it would later be known as the Oklahoma Territory until obtaining statehood in 1907. After the historic land run of 1889 and the opening of Native American lands, white settlers began to move in by the thousands. The numbers continued to grow after the second land run in 1892, and with the opening of the Cheyenne and Arapaho land in 1901, numbers continued to flourish.

In 1865, Jesse Chisholm developed a cattle trail that was used by Texas ranchers to drive cattle overland, from his southern trading post near the Red River to his northern trading post near Kansas City, Kansas. This would become known as the famous Chisholm Trail. This trail would help the territory grow and expand and help to build the state of Oklahoma.

In 1867, the United States and the Plains Indians negotiated the Treaty of Medicine Lodge, which would relocate the Cheyenne and Arapaho from Colorado to the Canadian County area. In 1870, the Cheyenne-Arapaho Agency was formed; it would later be known as the Darlington Agency, named after its first Indian agent.

After the Battle of the Washita in 1868, President Grant's Peace Policy made a profound change in Indian-white relations. A Quaker by the name of Brinton Darlington was appointed agent of the Upper Arkansas Agency. Darlington's strong convictions in his faith caused him to adhere to the Peace Policy. He would travel into the interior of the Indian Territory without military escort.

The military and the Cheyenne soon reached an agreement on the location of the new agency. The new location was in the North Canadian River area.

In May 1880, the first Mennonite missionary arrived at the mission. Samuel S. Haury and his bride, Susie L. Hirschler Haury, were the first to begin the "foreign" mission work. This was to be the first General Conference of the Mennonites of North America. When they first arrived, their home was not ready for them. Once they could move into their new home, they had very little in the way of furniture or even food. They were often visited by the Indians and were even receiving meals from them. Powder Face and Cut Finger, both Arapaho chiefs, made frequent visits, since they could speak and understand some English. Haury used the opportunity to learn Arapaho words.

While Haury lived as a missionary among the Cheyenne and Arapahos, the military occupied Fort Reno, only a few miles away. The cavalry and infantry that were stationed at the fort would soon play an important role in the transition of the area from Indian Territory to statehood in 1907. The troops of Fort Reno would also play an important part in evicting "Boomers" from the Unassigned Lands of the Indian Territory prior to the land run of 1889. They would later assist in the land run and help quell the political dispute among the "Five Civilized Tribes."

Canadian County has played host to an array of historical events, both good and bad. From the hard life of early settlers and cattle rustlers to outlaws and the persecution of the American Indians, it's no wonder the lands and cities retain such paranormal activity.

THE CHISHOLM TRAIL

We can't talk about Canadian County without talking about the Chisholm Trail. After all, the Chisholm Trail helped the Oklahoma Territory become a state. The Chisholm Trail was used to drive cattle overland. It stretched from Texas to Kansas, crossing through Oklahoma. Part of the trail is in Canadian County. The trail was named after Jesse Chisholm, even though Chisholm was not a cattleman or cowboy. Chisholm was, in fact, a frontier trader. He was, however, much more than just a simple trader.

Jesse Chisholm was born in 1805 of Cherokee and Scottish descent. He first moved to the Oklahoma Territory with his mother during the voluntary migration time. In 1826, Chisholm made his way toward present-day Wichita, Kansas, blazing a trail in search of gold. Over the next several years, he would become part of several expeditions, including the Dodge-Leavenworth Expedition. This group was the first to contact the southern Plains Indians on behalf of the United States federal government. In 1836, Chisholm married and settled in his father-in-law's trading post on the Little

River, where he worked in the Indian trade. Due to his ability to speak several different Native American languages, Chisholm became an interpreter and general aide. He was essential in helping the government negotiate treaties between the Republic of Texas and local Indian tribes. His diplomatic work spanned twenty years, during which time he continued in the Indian trade.

During the Civil War, many residents of the Indian Territory feared that they might get massacred if either side contended for control of the area. Chisholm led a group of refugees to the western part of the territory. At the end of the war, Chisholm settled in present-day Wichita. He built up the old military and Indiana trail into a road capable of carrying heavy wagonloads to help with his trading business. Later, the Texas-to-Kansas cattle drives began to use the trail, and it was renamed the Chisholm Trail. On March 4, 1868, Chisholm died of food poisoning at his last camp near Left Hand Spring. He is buried in Blain County, leaving behind a long legacy of achievements. In 1974, Jesse Chisholm was inducted into the Hall of Great Westerners, where his legacy lives on.

DARLINGTON

The Cheyenne Nation

Between 1500 and 1700, the Cheyenne resided in the Minnesota area. During the 1700s, they began to migrate toward the Dakotas. Some bands chose to build villages along the rivers and grow crops while other bands adopted buffalo hunting as a way of life. These bands would go on to develop the tipi dwelling, which later would help form the American Indian image that is most often depicted in the film industry today.

The Cheyenne migrated east of the Black Hills of South Dakota, which left Cheyenne bands very diverse. It was there that the prophet Sweet Medicine obtained four covenants. The four covenants were not to steal, not to kill, not to lie and not to commit incest. With these covenants, he helped organize the military societies and establish a judicial system. In doing so, Sweet Medicine created the Cheyenne Nation to be sovereign and independent.

The Cheyenne was a small nation made up of about three thousand people during that time. With the Kiowa pressing in and from the south and the Shoshone pressing in from the Great Plains to the west, the Cheyenne soon joined forces with their Arapaho allies to form a military force capable of keeping out any neighboring tribes. Despite their strong military force, the Cheyenne's biggest threat would soon come from the encroaching Americans.

In 1865, at the close of the American Civil War, the Cheyenne Nation was split in half due to the migration traffic along the Oregon and Santa Fe Trails. The Cheyenne Nation would become known as the Northern and Southern Cheyenne Nations. With the northern group heading north to Montana, the Southern Cheyenne ended up in Oklahoma along with their Arapaho allies. Between 1830 and 1870, there was a series of treaties with the U.S. government followed by episodes of warfare. From the massacre of noncombatant Cheyenne by the U.S. forces at Sand Creek, Colorado, in 1864 to the victory for the Cheyenne at the Battle of Little Bighorn in 1876, the Cheyenne way of life was about to change forever.

THE ARAPAHO TRIBE

During the 1700s, the Arapaho started to enter the northern plains. They were located south of the fork of the Saskatchewan River to western South Dakota and eastern Colorado. They were well known for trade of horses and goods and soon became the middlemen of trade along the Missouri River. In 1811, the Arapaho allied with the Cheyenne. This increased their hunting territory and helped to strengthen their army. Trading and hunting would be prosperous until the American migrants started heading west in search of land and gold.

The Fort Laramie Treaty of 1851 guaranteed the Arapaho the use of their range in Colorado. In 1861, the Southern Arapaho exchanged that territory for a reservation at Sand Creek in Colorado. Conflict soon arose between the Arapaho and the eastern Americans as miners and settlers began to trespass on Arapaho land. Tension arose on each side as the conflict developed for control of the Great Plains east of Colorado. In 1864, the commanding officer of Fort Lyon, Colonel John Chivington, invited the chiefs to hunt near Sand Creek. On November 29, 1864, Colonel Chivington and a group of Colorado volunteers attacked the unsuspecting village of Native Americans, slaughtering men, women and children. They mainly massacred women and children, and they also returned to kill the injured and mutilate their bodies.

In 1867, the Medicine Lodge Treaty was signed, guaranteeing the Arapaho a reservation in Kansas, but the location was rejected by the Arapaho. In 1869, the Arapaho and Cheyenne accepted a reservation in Indian Territory along the Canadian River. During the 1870s, there were approximately 1,500 Arapaho on the reservation. As game depleted, the

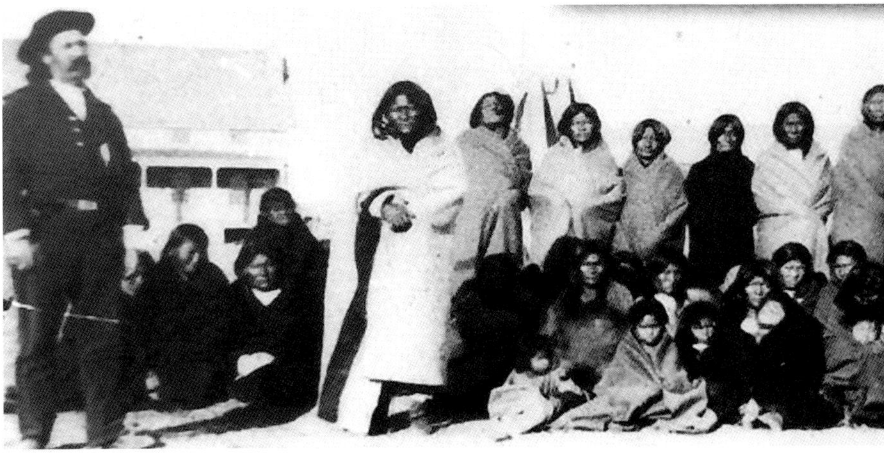

George Armstrong Custer with Arapaho Indians. *Courtesy of the Fort Reno Museum.*

Arapaho began relying on wage work and rations from their agent at the Darlington Agency. Left Hand, Bird Chief, Big Mouth, Little Raven and Powder Face were some of the chiefs who represented the Arapaho interest not only to the agent but to Washington, D.C., as well. The chiefs often reassured the U.S. government that they were loyal and would send their children to school if the government would abide by the treaties.

Economic conditions began to deteriorate on the reservation. In 1889, the Cheyenne-Arapaho agent began leasing tribal land to cattlemen. This caused a decline in Indian herds. Malnutrition and poverty soon caused an increase in human mortality among the Native Americans. In 1892, each Arapaho received a 160-acre allotment. Surplus land on the reservation was soon opened to settlers. The government paid the Arapaho and Cheyenne forty cents an acre, far less than the land's value. In 1902, Congress passed the Dead Indian Land Act, allowing the original land allotment to be sold when the allotter died. By the late 1920s, the Arapaho had lost 68 percent of their land.

The Cheyenne-Arapaho Nation

In 1937, under the Oklahoma Indian Welfare Act, the Cheyenne and Arapaho tribes organized an elective government known as the Cheyenne-

Arapaho Tribes of Oklahoma. They worked to regain their lands that the government still held. They worked on a low budget of leasing the tribal lands until the mid-1950s, when the tribal land started to produce oil.

The Cheyenne-Arapaho government grew after the Self-Determination Act of 1975. New business enterprises such as bingo halls, cigarette sales and casinos helped to sustain the budget. A business committee of eight tribal members met in a business setting to control the budget and function fully as their own government.

I was privileged enough to be welcomed into one of these meetings and obtained permission to write about them in this book. As I sat there quietly, I couldn't help but think about the long journey their people have made and the sacrifices they've had to endure over the past two hundred years. Through war, massacres and starvation, their people have survived. They sit before me a strong, proud nation that continues to fight for its people, its land and its customs. They honor their heritage and their ancestors, never forgetting their past and continuing to preserve their future. Remains of years gone by are still scattered throughout the land, memories soaked in emotions and blood powered by the sound of a beating drum and song carried on the wind. History lives on in the Cheyenne-Arapaho Nation.

THE DARLINGTON MENNONITE MISSION

In May 1880, the first Mennonite, Samuel S. Haury, and his bride, Susie L. Haury, arrived at Darlington to begin their missionary work with the Cheyenne-Arapaho Tribe. Life was not easy for the missionary workers. When they arrived, their home was not ready for them to move into. Until the house was complete, they had to stay with Agent John D. Miles, a Quaker missionary, and his wife. Soon they would move into their new home, but due to their belongings not arriving until later, they slept on the floor and made furniture out of boxes.

The main missionary goal was to teach the native Arapaho children, who were at that time in government schools, and from them bring the adults into Christianity. With their arrival being so late in the school year, the Haurys soon found themselves being visited daily by the Indians and often sharing meals with them. Two of the Arapaho chiefs, Powder Face and Cut Finger, made frequent visits since they understood some English. Haury would utilize these visits to learn some Arapaho words to help him with his teaching and Sunday services.

In the fall of 1881, the mission building was complete. It consisted of a kitchen, dining room, school room and several private rooms. There were also two dormitories in the garret. With this, the missionaries started holding school in their own building. By August, thirteen students had been accepted into the school, and several more were turned away due to the lack of clothing and supplies; in addition, the government school had to be filled first. The children were taught basic English; the boys were taught farming and the girls were taught housekeeping and needlework. Their main goal was to continue teachings of Christianity and its principles.

On February 19, 1882, a very cold and stormy night, the mission burned down, claiming the lives of four small children. Among the four were three half-Indian, half-white children by the names of Jenny, Walter and Emil. The fourth was the Haurys' own child at the tender age of nine months. Samuel Haury would go on to say, "What my heart felt with a look at these four little corpses and everything that was connected, I am not able to say. One must be led in such depths of sorrow and pain in order to grasp it."

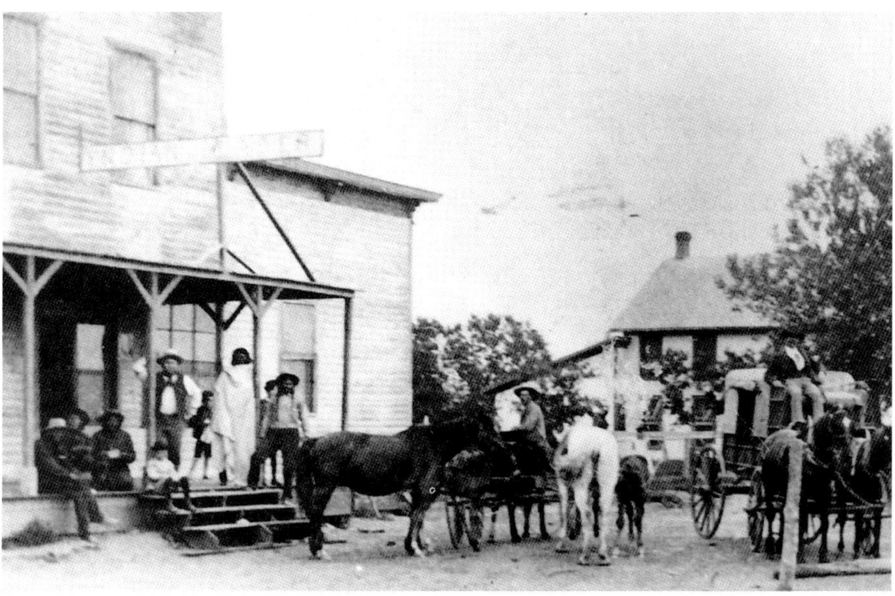

Darlington stagecoach stop. *Courtesy of the Fort Reno Museum.*

Even though the Haurys lost everything in the fire, the mission did not stop there. The school was continued in tents, and later, a new building was made from brick. In December 1882, the new mission was completed.

In 1884, a new agent by the name of Daniel B. Dyer was appointed to the Cheyenne-Arapaho Agency. He showed a harsher attitude toward the Indians. In one report, he was quoted as saying, "Conform to the will of the Government or take the consequences." He felt he lacked the power to "control" the Indians and thought they should be given swift punishment for wrongdoings. He would often praise the schools controlled by the Mennonite Society while talking down about the government schools.

In the early 1890s, major changes in personnel at Darlington began to take place. It was a critical time for the agency. Student numbers had begun to drop due to the opening of farmland for the Arapaho. The Indians' focus was now on their allotments and the settling on the land. Despite the agent's threats of withholding their rations, the Indians persisted in making a new home for themselves on their own land, thus decreasing the number of students at the missionary school. In June 1898, the Darlington Mennonite Mission was closed, never to open again.

In 1909, the land was purchased by Masons, and a Masonic home for children was built on the property. In 1913, a chapel was built by the Masons that still stands today. Starting in 1923, the Oklahoma Narcotics Institution resided on the land until 1932, when the Oklahoma Wildlife Department acquired it. The Oklahoma Wildlife Department stayed on location until 1996. The land, now owned by Redlands College, is used as part of its agriculture projects. Please remember that this is private property and that you must obtain permission from the college to go on-site. It is considered trespassing, and you can incur fines.

The two buildings rumored to be haunted are the mission and the old dormitories. The mission, a Spanish-style building constructed in 1913, stands tall with its white walls reaching up toward the blue skies of Oklahoma. It is rumored to house the spirit of a young lady in white often seen walking throughout the building. No one seems to know who she is or why she is there, but people often report a feeling of sadness when she appears.

The dormitories, with their faded and chipped paint, contain a different energy all their own. With window and doors boarded up, one can only guess if it is to keep someone out or something in. It is rumored that this building was once used as an orphanage where children were often mistreated and abused. It has also been said that it was used as a drug rehab site. People have reported seeing strange lights in and around the building. Others have

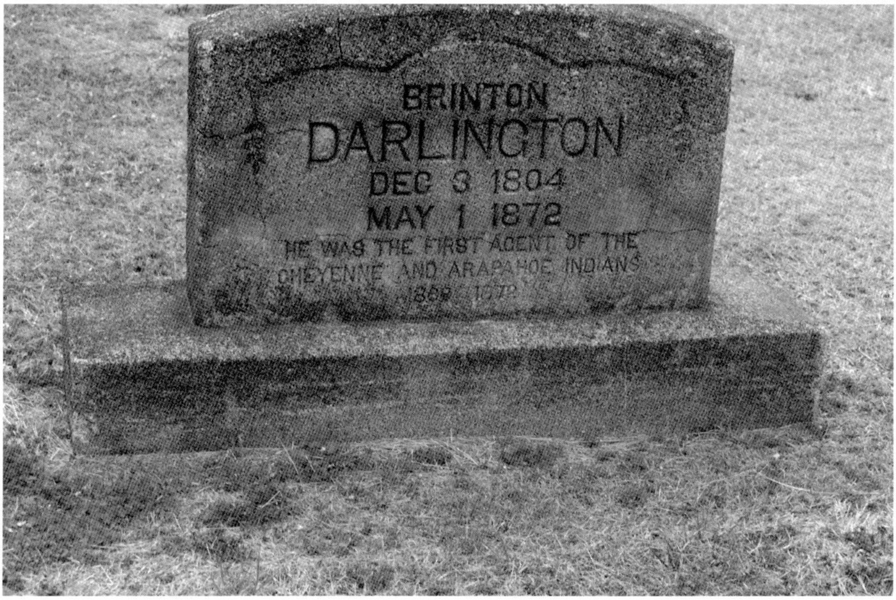

Brinton Darlington's grave. *Courtesy of Tanya McCoy.*

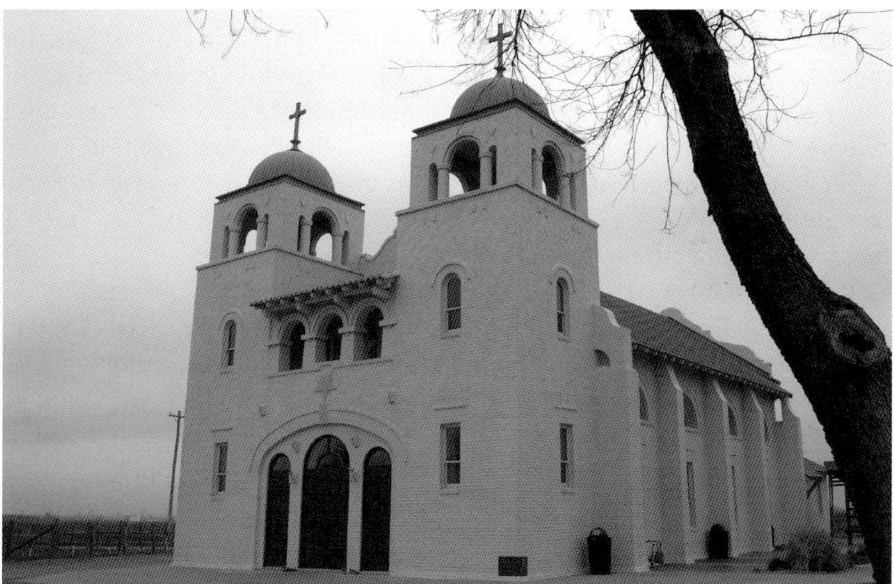

Darlington Mission. *Courtesy of Tanya McCoy.*

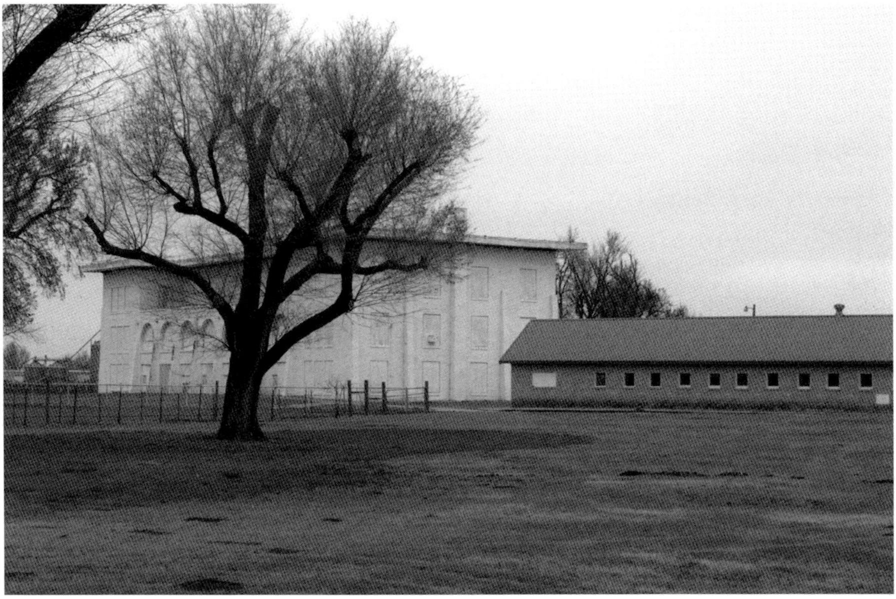

Darlington rehab dormitories. *Courtesy of Tanya McCoy.*

reported hearing screams coming from the decaying walls. What happened on this site to cause such misery to remain so many years after? Do the children remain after perishing so suddenly on that cold winter night over a century ago? Does the woman in white still search for a long-lost love or suffer from a broken heart? Or was she one of the missionaries who traveled here to share her faith? Between the mistreatment of American Indians, tuberculosis (better known as consumption in their day), malnutrition and starvation, which took the lives of many young children as well as adults, this land is soaked with memories and blood of years gone by. We may never know the identities of the spirits that remain or why they choose to do so. We can only hope that one day they might find peace and cross over to join their loved ones on the other side.

CONCHO

Concho, named after the Spanish word for Indian agent Charles E. Shell, is located just north of El Reno, Oklahoma, just off Highway 81. Its first post office opened on April 20, 1915, and the area is now home of the Cheyenne-Arapaho Tribes of Oklahoma.

After the closing of the Darlington Agency, a new boarding school was built. In 1909, the new Concho Boarding School opened its doors to welcome the Cheyenne-Arapaho children. The children were taught farming and basic life skills, much the same as they were at Darlington. This way of life was not easy for the children. They were set into a strict schedule. They were up for breakfast by 5:00 a.m. and were to be in class by 6:00 a.m. The first half of their day was spent in the classroom, learning subjects such as reading, writing and arithmetic. The second part of their day was spent doing labor. The boys would work in the fields and were taught farming and hunting. The girls were taught domestic duties, such as cleaning, cooking and sewing. Children were often punished if they were caught speaking in their native tongue or referring to their ancestral way of life. The punishment was swift and strict. Infractions called for one hour of hard labor. Their hair was cut and their clothes were changed to the point of trying to erase any signs of their tribal life. This was done due to a statement made by Captain Richard H. Pratt on the education of Native Americans in 1892: "Kill the Indian, and the man." He believed that in order to save the man, the Indians would need to renounce their tribal ways, convert to Christianity and seek out employment and education among the "best class" by leaving their reservation and cultural ways. Native

American children would often be taken and imprisoned at these schools. They were exposed to disease, sexual assault, abuse and murder, and some even committed suicide. Pratt became associated with the Americanization of the Native Americans by force that would later become known as the cultural genocide of the Native Americans.

The school continued to teach throughout the Great Depression despite the dust bowl, tornados and flash floods. President Franklin Roosevelt created the Executive Order of 1933, which authorized the Indian Services to establish a Civilian Conservation Corps camp to help control soil erosion, develop water resources and improve the buildings on the Concho grounds. Agency buildings were razed and restored in 1933, and a new hospital was constructed in 1941.

Economic crisis hit once more. Between 1940 and 1960, the Indian Termination Policy posed a threat to close the tribal school system. Where once the U.S. government sought to force the Native Americans into its school system and way of life, it now sought to end it due to financial worries. Tribal leaders fought against it, even sending pleas to the Oklahoma legislature to help fight against school closings. Their pleas were heard. In 1962, a new system was established. The new system was formed to help stream troubled students back into the school system. A new school complex was soon built, as well as dormitories for the students. This victory was short-lived. Just

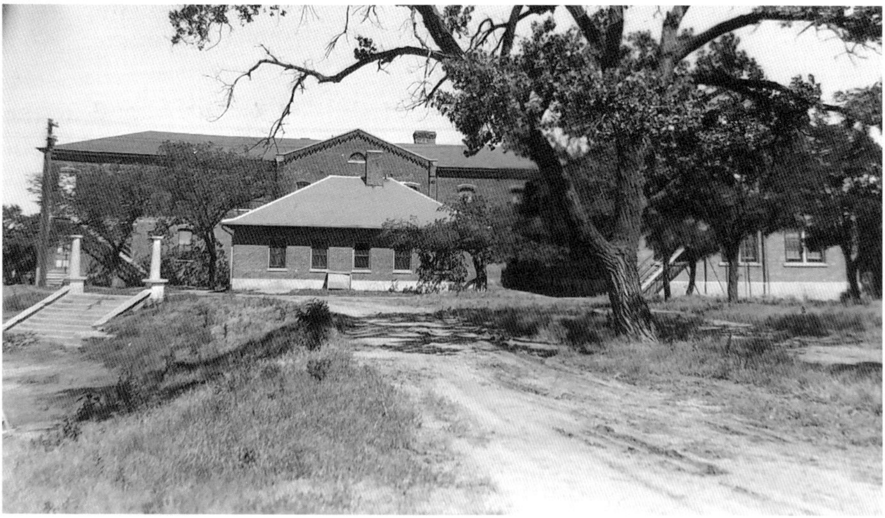

Old Concho Indian school. *Courtesy of the Cheyenne-Arapaho Nation.*

twenty years after the building of the new school, it closed its doors forever due to federal budget cuts.

General Philip Sheridan was said to have a different outlook on the Native Americans. He was later quoted as saying, "The only good Indians I have ever saw were dead ones." His statement later led to several massacres of Native Americans. He later denied making this statement, but his actions still spoke his words. Sheridan and Lieutenant Colonel George A. Custer led the Battle of Washita River on November 27, 1868, when they attacked the Cheyenne, Kiowa and Comanche at their winter campgrounds. They took their winter supplies of food and livestock, killing any who resisted. Many were driven back onto the reservation. General Sheridan was appointed commander of the Great Plains area, and he allowed professional hunters to trespass on Indian land. He was quoted as saying, "Let them kill, skin and sell until the buffalo are exterminated." By 1874, more than four million bison had been butchered, leading to the starvation and malnutrition of the Indians.

Today, Concho is a small area consisting of a few buildings, offices, a library, farmland, a gas station and a casino. Most people relate Concho to the Lucky Star Casino, but just down the road is the heart of Concho, filled with the history of a proud Indian nation and its people. As you pass the casino, you find yourself driving down a long, paved road lined with trees that look out into the empty pastures where the tall Oklahoma grass grows. If you are lucky, you might even see a small family of bison grazing in the fields or a coyote on the hunt. If you're really lucky, you may even get a glimpse of Bigfoot roaming around.

On one of my recent visits to Concho, I was visiting with Max Bear, the culture heritage program director, when he told me the tale of the Bigfoot sighting at Concho. In 2002, a security officer who was working at the Lucky Star Casino noticed something strange on the security tapes. What he described was a tall creature with fur out behind the building by the grease trap and trash can area. He watched the creature walk away out into the pasture area and soon followed suit. He was unable to locate the creature but did find some large footprints—much larger and wider than a human would make—with the toes, foot pad and heel print intact. He made a cast of one and even took several other people out to see them. Several kitchen workers have also reported seeing the creature around the trash cans. They report always feeling like they were being watched, or they would hear a strange whistling noise coming from that area. Troy Hudson has been researching Bigfoot since 2004. He has conducted several investigations and interviews in that area. He believes there could very well be a Sasquatch in the area based on his research and reports. Years later, while out in the neighboring woods, Max stated that he found a small dug-out area in the ground with what appeared to be two places to sit in it. Was this possibly where the Sasquatch lived, or was it simply a man-made spot for men to hide in while hunting? Children have reported seeing the creature in various areas as well as knocking on their windows at night. Could a Sasquatch be roaming the native land, or is it perhaps more? According to Troy, throughout his many years of study, he has often "seen a lot of the paranormal stuff get identified more coming from the big guys and vice versa."

As you travel farther down the long stretch of road, you will come to the end of the tree line. The minute you arrive, you can feel a shift in the energy field. My first visit to the Concho Indian School was interesting, to say the least. The minute I hit the energy field, I felt a headache coming on. Our host, Calvin White, founder of JPS (Just Paranormal Stuff), out of the El Reno/Concho area, led us down to the buildings of the Concho Indian School, along with Kale Epperson and his team, Paranormal Investigations of Oklahoma.

Empty shells of buildings lined the gray stormy skies; doors and windows were missing from the structures that once housed the schoolchildren of the tribe. As we exited our vehicles, raindrops began to fall from the darkening sky as the clouds swirled softly above our heads. In the close distance, we could hear the steady beat of the tribal drums, the sound of thunder farther off in the distance. The smell of the fresh rain hitting the soft dirt filled our nostrils, and a chill was carried on the breeze. We knew this was going to be an interesting night.

The first building he led us to was the old hospital/rehab area. Its exterior walls housed multiple window frames with broken or empty glass. Just above the front entryway was an open rooftop, which sheltered the way in. I was drawn to a window to my left on the second floor. There I could sense a male presence. He appeared to be a middle-aged man. He seemed angry and sad as I noticed him step out of the window onto the ledge. Then he was gone. As we walked into the building, we had to be careful where we stepped. Broken glass, wood, nails and other metals all lined the floors and walls. The interior walls have begun to crumble due to the years of rain and neglect. Nature has taken its toll on the building. We decided to start an EVP recording in the room where I had previously seen the male apparition. We set up recorders and opened our equipment case. We set out several Parascopes and grabbed our mel meters (EMF detector). With our Ghost Radio app going, we began to ask our questions. Not long into the investigation, we began to get hits on the Parascope. We received many responses that would relate directly to the use of the building. While standing out in the hall, you could look clear into the second building due to the lack of doors. While two of us looked over, we both saw what appeared to be a full-body apparition move from one room to the other. It was still light enough outside that we knew it could not simply be the light playing tricks on us. A group of us walked over to investigate the location while others watched us leave. We searched the building, but no one could be found—at least no one living—and no one had been seen leaving the building as we approached.

Our next visit was over to an abandoned duplex. At one spot, the wooden floor had completely caved in, leaving the wood lying scattered several feet below on the dirt floor. Birds had made nests along the walls and the empty door frames, with their hatchlings chirping out to their mothers in search of food. Shadows could be seen scurrying along the walls as if a game of hide-and-seek were afoot. Lightning began to shoot across the sky, and we found ourselves patiently waiting as the sky suddenly opened and a heavy rain began to fall. We continued with our investigation in the building, again running our recorders and various pieces of equipment. We witnessed a few Parascope hits and a few shadows, but nothing much else was noticed.

We traveled on to the dormitories, one for the boys and one for the girls. With no doors to open or hold us back, we entered the first dorm. It, too, was falling apart due to the weather and mother nature taking control. Walls were stripped, leaving the structure boards exposed. Old wires hung from the ceilings and walls. Plants had begun to creep in and line the inside of the old building. The falling walls seemed heavy, as if laden with sadness and grief. You could almost feel the emotions coming from the walls themselves. The girls' dorm is reported to have a lot of paranormal activity, from pieces of ceiling tiles being thrown and people getting hit to a photo of a full-body apparition standing at the end of the hall.

The second dorm is located just south of the building. Its state is just the same—no windows, no doors, along with several open areas leaving it exposed to mother nature's wrath. This dorm is different though. Inside and along some of the outside is beautiful Native American art, giving the building a unique life of its own. Along with the artwork are several poems and statements written by their creator to express the suppression they must have been feeling toward a government that had shunned their people for so long. These dorms were built in 1962, more recently than the original Concho Indian School.

To get to the original Concho school, you must take a drive across the creek to the site where the buildings once stood, now just a pile of concrete and mortar. This is the area where the children of the Cheyenne-Arapaho would have suffered the most at the hands of those who were "led to reform the savages." Nothing short of slavery and abuse was used to reform their children, as was ordained by the U.S. government at the time, as well as various religious groups doing missionary work in the area. Various investigators have reported seeing orbs (balls of light) moving quickly through the area. Calvin White shared an experience he and his team witnessed one evening while investigating the old bridge area. The bridge is the old crosswalk bridge that separates the old school from the employee housing area. "There were four of us there, and we heard this swooshing sound that came in front of us. It went to the woods first and came back through. It was so fast and forceful that it moved sticks and leaves on the ground." He grabbed his camera and snapped a photo. A bright orange orb is noted in the shot. There have also been reports of people hearing children laughing and playing in the woods around the area when no children are present.

Another place of interest is building one. It is said that it could very well be the most haunted building on the property. It is currently the oldest building, dating back to the 1800s. It is now used as an office building.

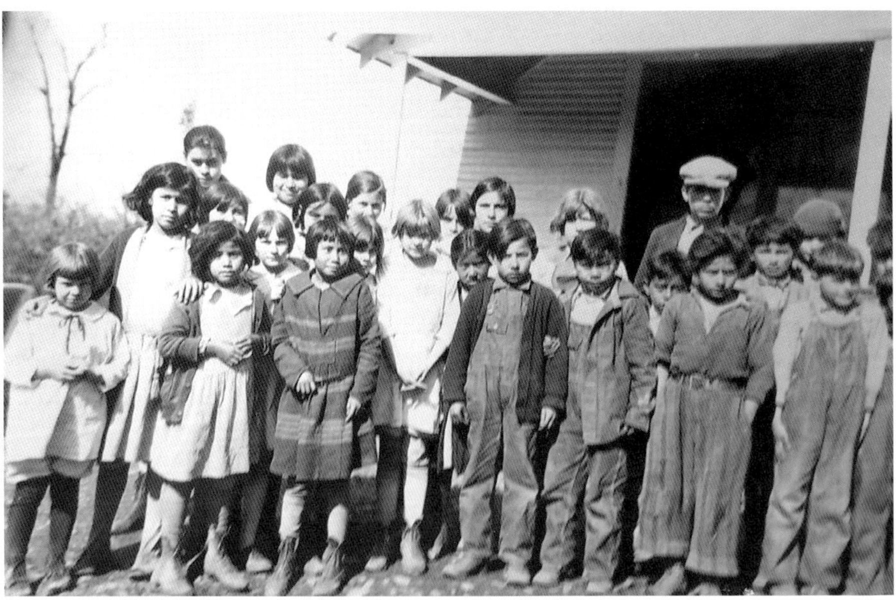

Cheyenne-Arapaho Indian school. *Courtesy of the Cheyenne-Arapaho Nation.*

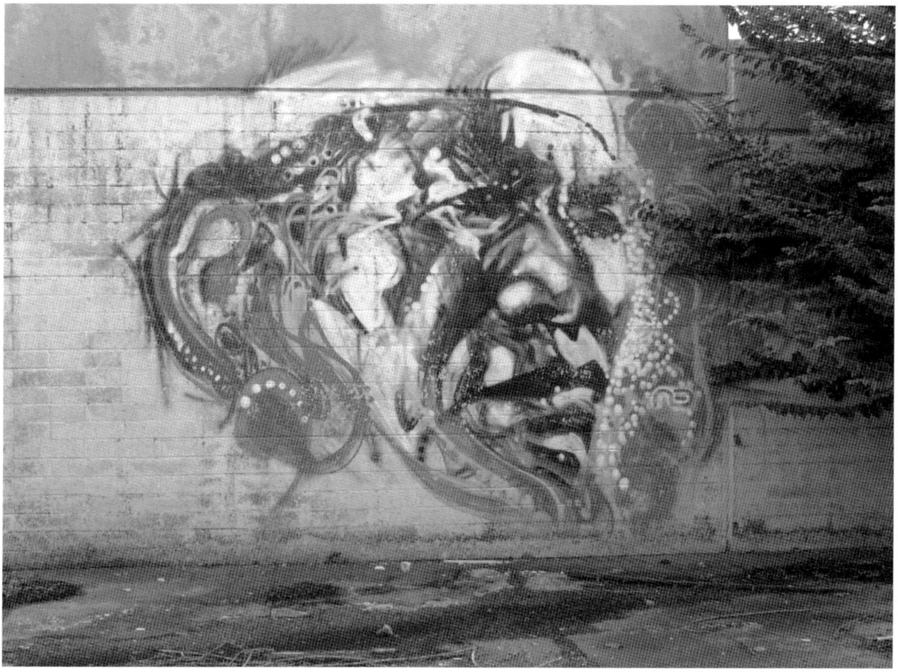

Native American artwork at the Concho boarding school. *Courtesy of Whitney Wilson.*

There have been many reports of people seeing the spirit of a young boy in and around the building. One night, a security officer was driving around the building when he noticed something in one of the windows. He stopped and took a picture of it. When he looked at the picture, he noticed the face of a little boy looking back at him. He quickly left. The little boy has also been seen running across the open yard area between the buildings. Max Bear shared his own personal experience with the little boy. He states he was sitting out in the yard waiting on some of his friends when he saw a small boy wearing a red-checkered shirt run from the clinic area to the dormitories and then simply disappear. Many believe it is the spirit of a young Indian boy who passed away many years ago. Not far from building one is a dirt road that travels across the small creek. Just a few yards back into the woods is a low-lying area where the creek would gather up, causing a small pond to form. During the winter months, the pond would freeze over, and the children would go there to ice-skate. Legend has it that one day a little boy fell through some thin ice and passed away. Many feel that this is the spirit of the little boy and that he continues to haunt the area to this day.

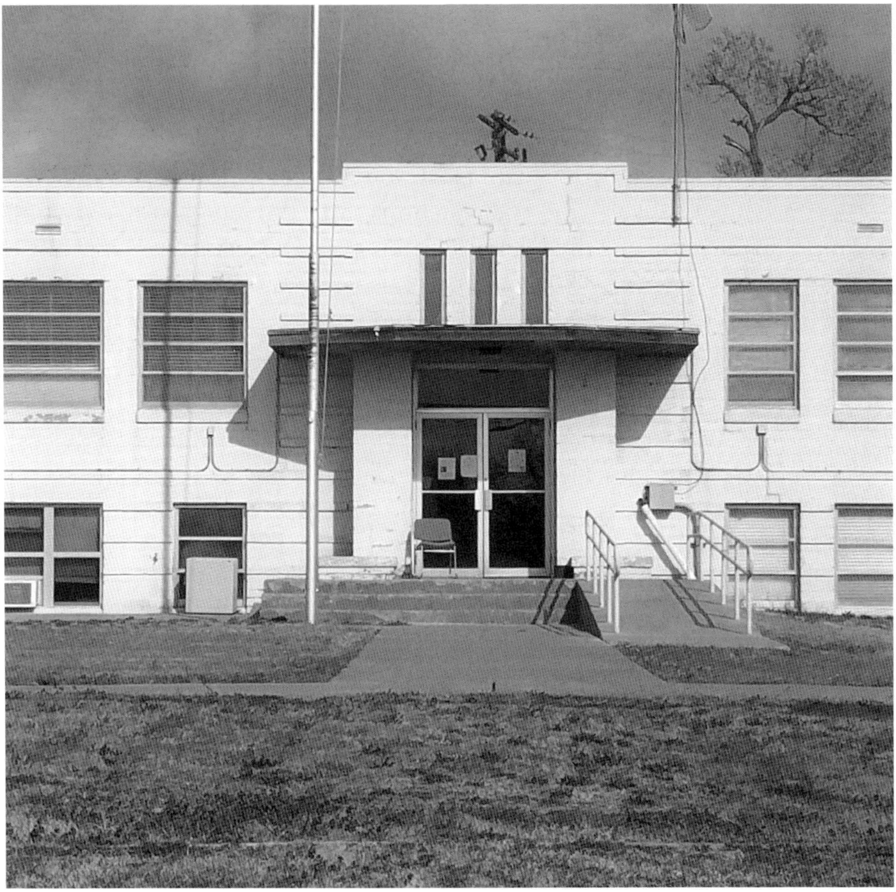

Building at Concho. *Courtesy of Tanya McCoy.*

The next building of interest is the basement of the more recent school building. The spirit of a little girl is most often seen there. The night we went, we set up boo-bear (a trigger object constructed to detect EVPs, touch and temperature changes and talk). It didn't take much time for something or someone to start to interact with the toy. Farther down the hall, we started to witness shadow figures and decided to set up one of our Parascopes in the area. Not long after, the Parascopes started to respond as if answering our questions. That night, we believe we were in contact with the spirit of a small female child who was curious but still scared and kept her distance. Calvin shared a story of one of his previous investigations at the same location. He also shared a picture he had taken that shows the image of a little girl. Could this have been the same little girl we were interacting with that night? If so, I would love to learn who she was and why she has chosen to stay. Perhaps this was the only home she had ever known, or perhaps she is simply lost. For her sake, I hope she finds peace one day and is reunited with those who love her.

From Bigfoot to ghostly apparitions, if you go looking for the paranormal here, you will very likely find it. Concho is land drenched in history and tradition. It is home to proud, mighty people who celebrate their past, present and future. They hold tribal ceremonies and powwows to honor their ancestors and even offer classes for those wishing to learn some of the trades of their people. Anyone wishing to learn more about the Cheyenne-Arapaho Nation, please visit their website (www.c-a-tribes.org) for more information. Please respect the tribe and do not trespass. Contact their offices to learn more.

El Reno

Fort Reno

During the Indian wars era in 1874, Fort Reno was established as a temporary military camp to protect the Cheyenne-Arapaho Agency at Darlington. The camp functioned as the "Camp Near the Cheyenne Agency" for five months shy of two years under Fifth Infantry and Sixth Cavalry soldiers prior to the expansion of the camp and naming of the fort. In February 1876, General Philip Sheridan named the permanent military post Fort Reno, honoring his close friend Major General Jesse L. Reno, of Virginia, who had been killed during the Civil War in 1863. Sheridan's headquarters, a small log cabin structure, now sits on the property of the Canadian County Historical Museum in El Reno.

Soldiers of the fort, including cavalry and infantry units, the buffalo soldiers, Cheyenne and Arapaho Indian scouts and U.S. Marshal service, were charged with policing the area of the unassigned lands prior to the land runs of 1889, 1892 and 1894. While the only battle near the fort was the Battle of Sand Hill in 1875, from 1892 to 1908, troops from Fort Reno were utilized in political disputes, the Spanish-American War in Cuba and rebellions among Indians, in addition to their role during the land runs. The fort ceased to function as an active military post in 1908.

In 1908, the same year the fort was closed as an active military base, it was reactivated by the U.S. Army as a remount station. The fort would now be

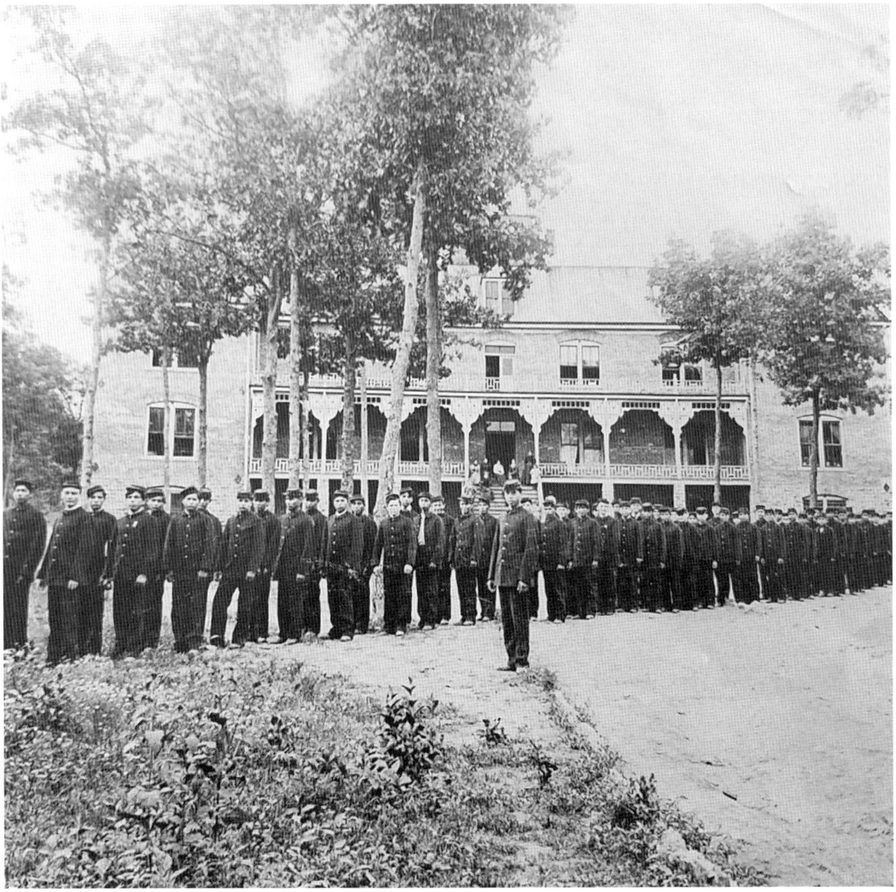

Historical troops of Fort Reno. *Courtesy of the Fort Reno Museum.*

used to train mules and horses for military duty. These service animals were trained for active duty and used in World Wars I and II and the Korean War. Trained horses and mules were also shipped to other countries to be used by Allied forces, oftentimes accompanied by Fort Reno remount troops. The fort grounds were also home to polo competitions, horse races, shows and auctions and some community activities. Following the end of World War II, Fort Reno was closed in 1948 and turned over to the USDA. It has since been the home of the USDA Grazinglands Research Laboratory, hosting the visitors' center/museum.

The visitors' center/museum is a remodeled officers' quarters that hosts hundreds of visitors each year. This two-story building is now the home to historical photos, service uniforms and weapons from the fort's functioning days. Visitors and staff have reported the feeling of being watched while in the building. If you stay long enough, you may hear the chatter of voices long passed or footsteps of an unseen visitor. Patrons have even reported feeling as if their hair was pulled as they tour the artifacts.

As the museum director of the Cavalry Museum, Wendy Ogden has spent many nights working after hours. One night in particular, her thirteen-year-old son was with her as she was finishing up the workday. The two left the museum at approximately eleven o'clock at night. As she drove down the road to leave the fort, her son was frantically telling her that something was in the middle of the road. Wendy didn't see anything and kept driving ahead as he called out, "Mom!" Her son let out a sigh of relief and said, "Thank God it stepped to the left." Wendy never saw anything in the road. As soon as they returned home, her son drew a picture of what he had seen: a man who appeared to have no arms, in military clothes. Later in the week, Wendy's son returned to the museum. There were reenactors practicing on the parade grounds. As her son watched the reenactors, he recognized the "at ease" posture of the soldiers as what he saw the night the man stood in the road. They traveled back to where he saw the man. The spot in the road where the apparition stood marked the location of the original gate to the fort. Perhaps a soldier's sense of duty never dies.

Located three miles west and two miles north of present-day El Reno, many of the original buildings are still standing today, some of which have been restored and are available to tour. The visitors' center/museum, Cavalry Museum, chapel and the Fort Reno Cemetery are open for public touring. Other structures on the property include officers' quarters, a Victorian-style home, a commissary/armory and a barn. Considering Fort Reno's history, it's no surprise that stories of unconventional visitors have arisen over the years—visitors whose names you won't find in a guest registration book but perhaps may see on a tombstone in the fort's cemetery.

The Welcome Center at Fort Reno

As you exit the highway and pass through the gates to head back toward the fort, you're met with open fields stretching on for mile after mile. Cattle graze nearby, and you might be lucky enough to see a large red-tailed hawk swooping down to catch its lunch. It's a rather peaceful place now—much different than what it must have been like so many years ago. From horse and buggy to military transport, Fort Reno has seen many people come and go through its gates over the past 143 years.

The first exercise of the fort was to police the Cheyenne-Arapaho reservation. Duty would call again during 1878, when the Northern Cheyenne arrived. In the late summer of 1878, after a long, harsh winter, many Cheyenne perished due to poor medical attention, inadequate food and disease at Darlington. Little Wolf, tired of the mistreatment of his people, went to agent John Miles to ask about leaving in hopes of returning to their homeland. His plea fell on deaf ears, and his request was denied. Little Wolf was quoted as saying to agent Miles, "Now listen to what I say to you, I am going to leave here; I am going north to my own country." During the late hours of the night, Chief Little Wolf and Chief Dull Knife led a band of Indians and fled from the reservation to head back north to their homeland. The troops of Fort Reno would now face a new challenge. Captain Joseph Rendlebrock, along with two cavalry troops, pursued the bands in an attempt to bring them back to the reservation. The cavalry troops were up for a long battle. Under the leadership of Little Wolf, the Cheyenne were able to keep their enemy at bay despite their limited numbers. Several battles were won by the Cheyenne due to Little Wolf's superior tactical leadership. Captain Rendlebrock would become well known for being the master of retreat and would later be court-martialed and dismissed from service.

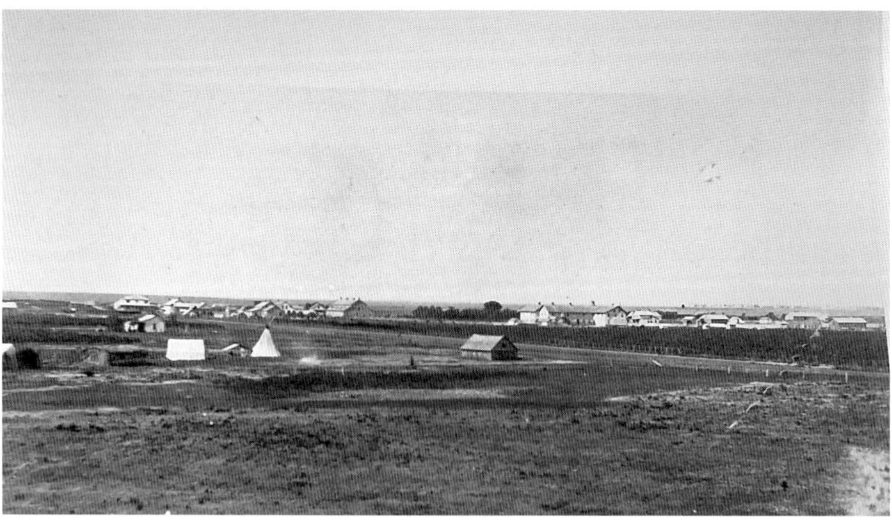

Historic Fort Reno. *Courtesy of the Fort Reno Museum.*

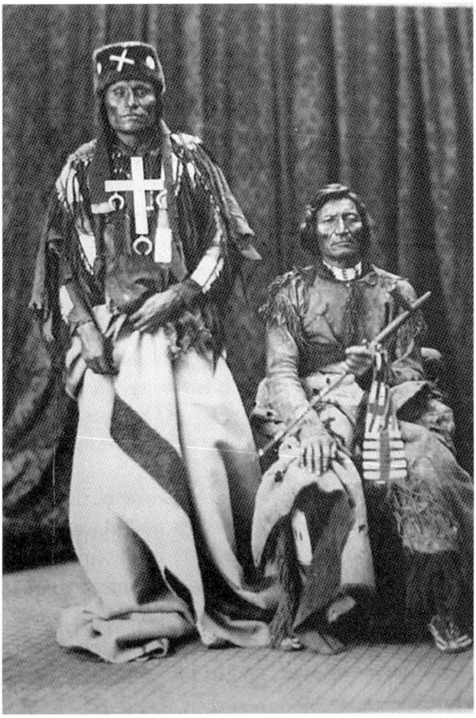

Left: Little Wolf (*left*) and Dull Knife. *Courtesy of the Cheyenne-Arapaho Nation.*

Below: Cheyenne soldiers. *Courtesy of the Fort Reno Museum.*

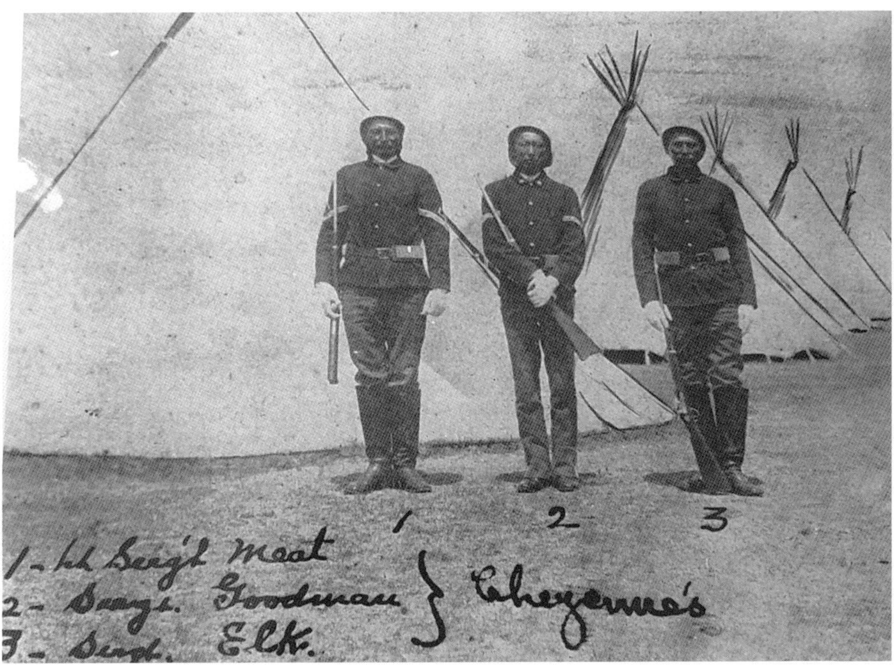

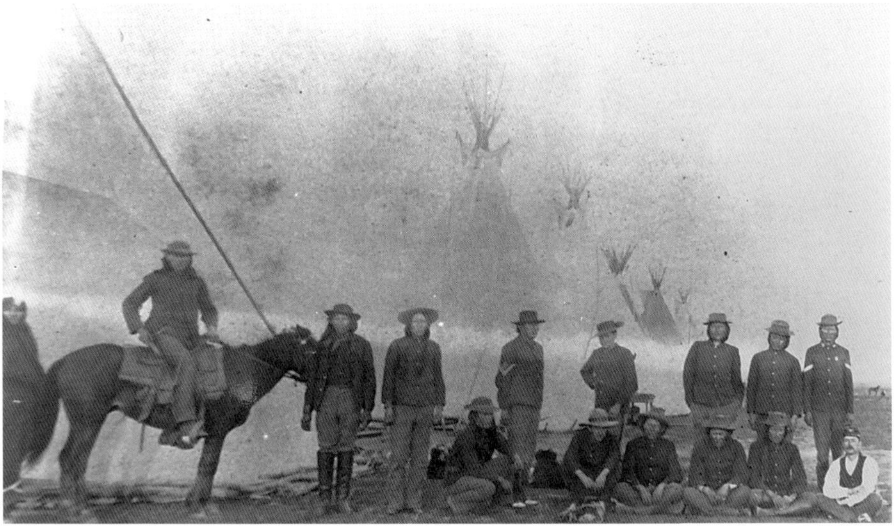

Indian scouts from Fort Reno. *Courtesy of the Fort Reno Museum.*

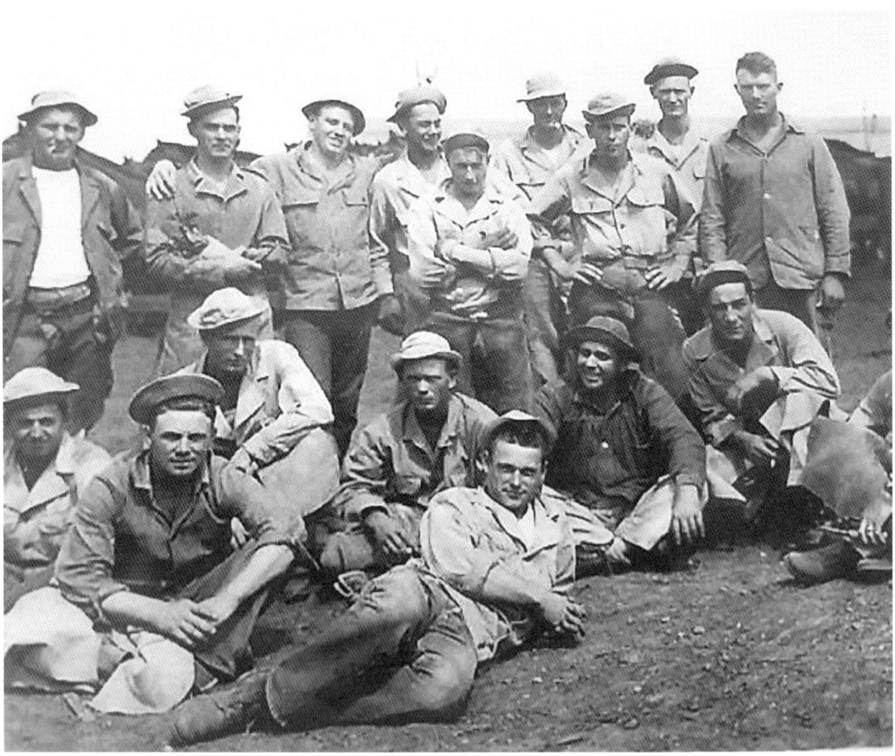

Fort Reno soldiers. *Courtesy of the Fort Reno Museum.*

Today, Fort Reno is open to tourists who wish to take a step back in time to see a little bit of what life would have been like for the cavalry during the Indian wars. The first building you come to after driving down the long entry road is the visitors' center. It is here that you will check in. It's a small whitewashed building built in 1936 with a small covered porch.

When you first enter the building, you are greeted with a small open reception area with a glass case full of small objects to purchase to help you remember your trip to the fort. Lining the walls are various books and goods telling some of the fort's past. Just off to the left you will notice a beautiful wooden staircase leading up to the second floor. As you walk toward the staircase, you come to an entryway. To the right sits a door leading down into the basement; the left leads to another open room area. In the room, you will find a large round table stacked with books and photo albums, open and ready to share some of Fort Reno's past.

As you ascend the winding staircase, you will enter a very narrow hallway. Wooden floors line all the rooms, and the creaking of the wood echoes throughout the building as you pass from one room to the next. Various artifacts are displayed around the building. From officers' boots and uniforms to even bunks, you can see how many officers would live from day to day in the building.

Jim Johnston has volunteered off and on for the fort since 1989. As a current member on the board, Jim spends his Tuesdays in the welcome

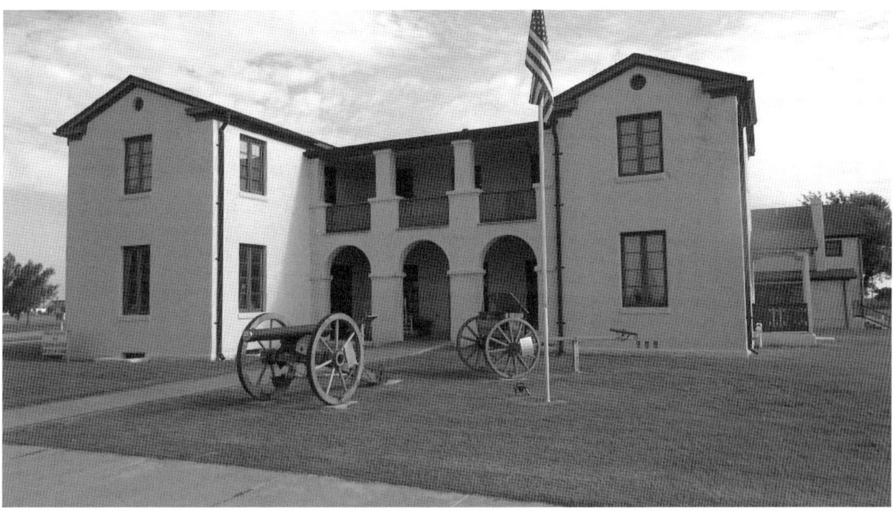

Fort Reno welcome center. *Courtesy of Tanya McCoy*.

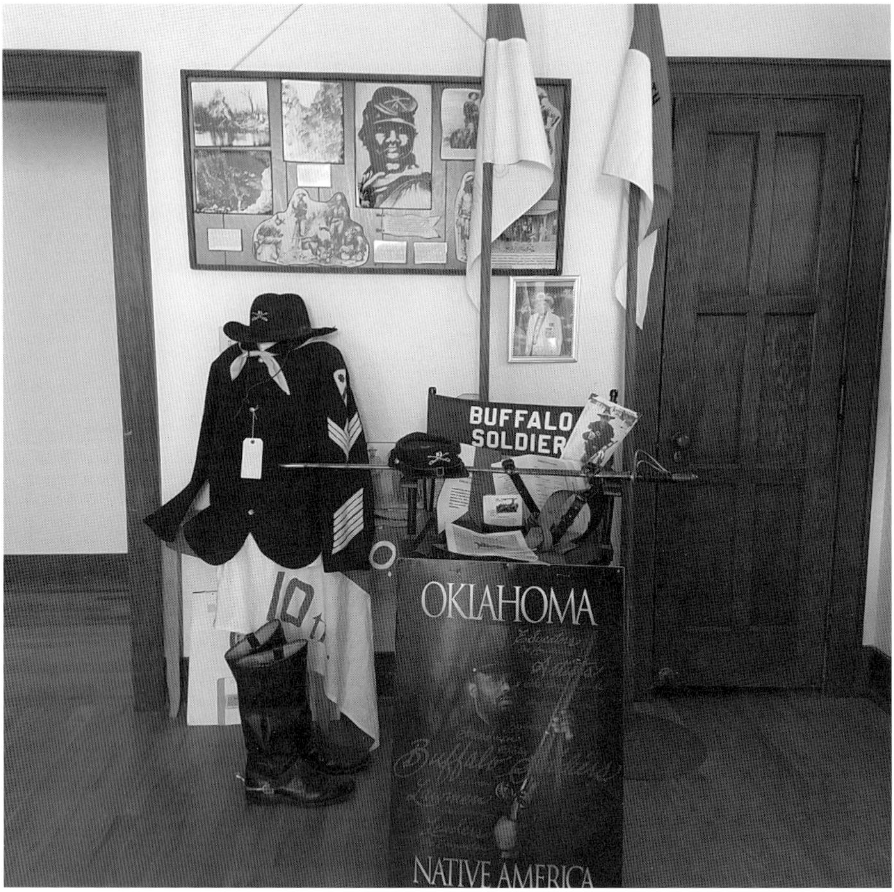

Upstairs in the Fort Reno welcome center. *Courtesy of Tanya McCoy.*

center. I asked Jim about the reports of paranormal activity in the building I had heard over the years of various encounters from other eyewitnesses. I was curious to know if he himself had had any experiences. Jim shared a few stories that he had been witness to throughout the other buildings around the fort. He shared one woman's experience that she had reported to him while visiting the center. She had been walking around the building looking at all the artifacts when she suddenly felt a forceful tug on her head. As she turned to see who was there, no one was to be seen. She quickly ran downstairs to report what had happened. Other reports over the years have been of hearing footsteps upstairs, as if made by the thumping of a heavy boot. Cold spots have been reported throughout the building, and people report the feeling of being watched. Many believe that the building is still haunted by a lieutenant colonel who supposedly committed suicide in the upstairs bathroom by shooting himself in the head. One story even states that repairs had to be made to patch the bullet hole in the ceiling.

Do soldiers still walk these narrow halls of the welcome center or pull the hair of unsuspecting visitors? Perhaps you yourself will have an experience of your own, should you choose to visit Fort Reno. It would definitely be a trip worth making to see.

THE CAVALRY MUSEUM AT FORT RENO

The present-day Cavalry Museum, open to visitors, is the oldest structure on Fort Reno grounds. It was originally built as a duplex for housing for officers and their families. The structure was lived in from 1876 to 1948 and then sat vacant for many years. Finally, in 2014, as the structure was nearing demolition, the U.S. Cavalry Association raised the funds to restore the building and opened it to the public in April 2015. The Cavalry Museum at Fort Reno is now the national headquarters for the U.S. Cavalry Association and houses items from saddles to service uniforms and many other service-related artifacts. The museum stands just east of the parade grounds and south of the visitors' center/museum. The restored two-story building features an enclosed porch that spans the entire front of the house. Upon entering, it is apparent that this building was restored with great care, from the original wood finishes to the artifacts displayed. As you enter the front of the building, you are greeted by a set of stairs that lead up to the second floor. Just to your right is the open archway, which leads into a large open room filled with artifacts and various memorabilia available for purchasing. You will also find your tour guide there ready to assist you or answer any questions you might have. When you start your tour, you are led upstairs and shown through various rooms. This building was once a duplex housing unit, and signs of that can be seen throughout the building. Each room holds its own theme or motif as it showcases items from the cavalry's past. From officers' living quarters to memorabilia from the Civil War, it truly is a step back in time.

During its vacancy, several reported some odd occurrences. A worker on site of Fort Reno reported seeing lights on in the building even though there was no electricity. When restoration began on the buildings, workers on the

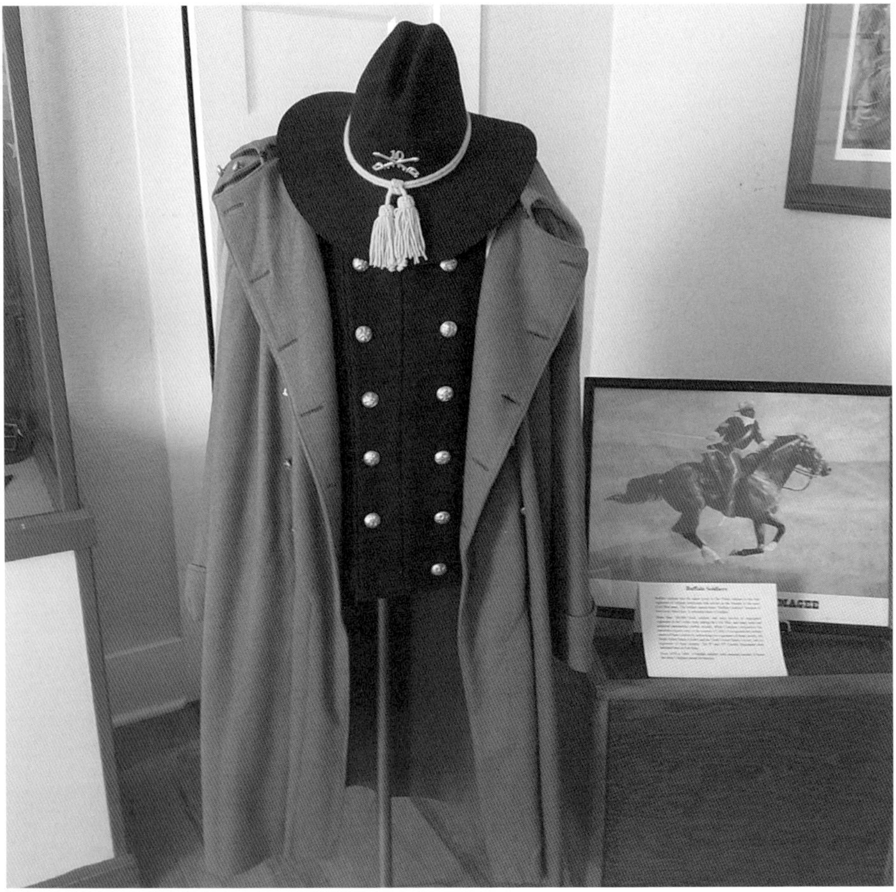

Union soldiers' Civil War costume at the Cavalry Museum at Fort Reno. *Courtesy of Tanya McCoy.*

outside of second-story windows reported seeing a lady walk through the hallway in front of them and vanish through a wall.

Wendy Ogden, director and curator of the museum, tells the story of when she first began work at the museum. The first day she was left alone, the fire alarms kept going off; this was not the usual chirp of a dying battery but a longer blip than that. After speaking with her boss, she was told the fire alarms do not even have batteries; they are hardwired into the house. After she acknowledged the activity, it stopped. Two others reported the same activity on their first day alone in the house and the ceasing of beeping after it was acknowledged as well.

On many occasions in between visitors and after hours, Wendy has felt the presence of a young child. Pencils have been knocked off desks, items have moved frequently at about waist level and a flask flew off a shelf late one night when her kids were working in the office area. A volunteer leading a tour for a small family felt he might be going crazy when he heard children laughing throughout the tour until the parents in the group asked him, "Do you hear kids laughing?" Burial records show that a young boy, Louis Trass, an officer's son, died in April 1900 of unknown causes. Maria Wheeler, the daughter of a widow, passed in a house fire in the home that used to stand just north of the museum; her brother survived. Louis and Maria are buried next to each other in the fort's cemetery.

On one occasion, a patron of the museum was so shaken by her experience during her visit that she drove to a diner in town to write down her experience and brought it back out to the museum. Wendy said everything was normal that day. The couple had come in and was walking through the upstairs at a normal pace when all of sudden they came running downstairs. The female visitor said she heard someone choking and swore it was Wendy behind her. She turned and asked, "Are you OK?" at which time she realized no one was behind her.

Wendy encounters many who claim to be psychics, mediums and sensitives. These visits can be interesting. On several occasions, however, the same topic has been mentioned: "Someone here is unhappy about an item in the museum." After a number of these type of encounters, a lady approached Wendy about the item. She offered to show the woman the item likely at the source of this entity's frustration, so the woman followed her to the saddle room. As the two women stood in front of a specific saddle, the straps began to sway on their own. This particular saddle was, in fact, not a cavalry saddle but one that an officer's daughter had used as part of a traveling circus. The traveling circus saddle is still in the museum.

Paranormal teams have visited this location with equipment and gotten EVPs, a fancy way of saying a recording of a voice other than those present in the room. Some nights, after hours, chatter can be heard, but one cannot make out the conversation. Ron Cross, founder of PROS Investigations, was in charge of one of the first paranormal teams to assist in the ghost tours held at the fort. Prior to the Cavalry Museum opening in the building, Ron's team had a chance to investigate it. He remembers one night he and two others were investigating the building when they decided to conduct the "knock test," where you knock a certain number of times or in a certain well-known tune and see if the spirit will answer back. That night, the spirit was happy to comply. He says they asked the spirit to knock three times and gave an example. Immediately after, they all heard the three knocks mere feet away from them. They tried the experiment again, only to receive the same response. Is this definite proof that this building is haunted? No, but it does open the door to wonder why and possibly who could have made those three loud knocks in response so many years ago.

Before visiting the museum, I had little information about it other than it's a cavalry museum and there's likely two children hanging around it. Upon arriving, I was invited to look around and get a feel for the building. While walking upstairs, I felt I did encounter a lady, an overseer of things she seemed like. While I was walking through the rooms a couple of times, there were footsteps in the room next to me, even though I was alone upstairs. I did not pick up on a young boy until a little later, as I was sitting in the office speaking with Wendy, my three-year-old pacing back and forth, oblivious to anything. He peeked out from the hallway across from us, almost as if he was curious. Are the spirits of this house trying to get our attention? Are they trying to give a message or just returning to a familiar spot? Perhaps a visit to the museum could help you answer those questions.

THE CHAPEL AT FORT RENO

Located just northwest of the welcome center sits an old European-style chapel, built in 1944 by a group of German prisoners of war. A shield of arms still graces the chapel today to remind everyone of the craftsmen who labored to build the chapel so many years ago.

On July 4, 1943, during World War II, the first German POWs arrived at Fort Reno by rail. Most of the prisoners were from General Rommel's Afrika Korps and were captured in North Africa. Prisoners were given various jobs around the fort; some were even hired out as farmhands to neighboring farms. The farmers would pay the government $1.50 a day for the prisoners' labor, and in turn, the government would pay the prisoners $0.10 an hour in scrip money for them to purchase various goods at the canteen. Prisoners were allowed far more luxury at the fort than American prisoners were in Germany. Prisoners at the fort were able to purchase two beers a day along with cigarettes and various other items. When prisoners left the fort to work on the farms, they would pack a sack lunch to take with them. Many of the farmers still provided food or snacks for them.

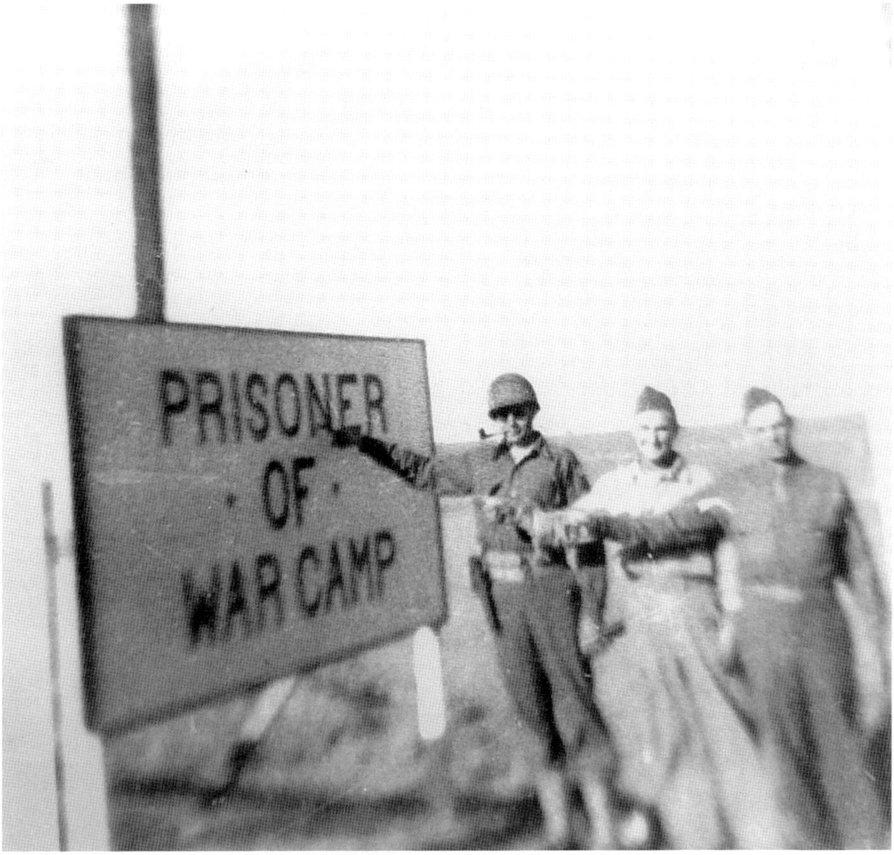

German prisoners of war. *Courtesy of the Fort Reno Museum.*

When some of them returned to Germany after the war, many of them still stayed in touch. There are around seventy German POWs buried at the cemetery but only one of those buried actually died at Fort Reno. The prisoners left an everlasting mark on Fort Reno. From the trees lining the entry drive to the beauty of the white chapel, Fort Reno shares a past of unity between the soldiers, the farmers and the POWs during a difficult time in our country's history.

As you arrive at the chapel, you are witness to the white contrast of the chapel walls against a light blue sky. The dark wooden doors with their cast-iron hinges and the square turret located on the east side of the building give the chapel a medieval feel. As you ascend the set of stairs and approach the heavy wooden set of doors, get ready to take a step back in time as

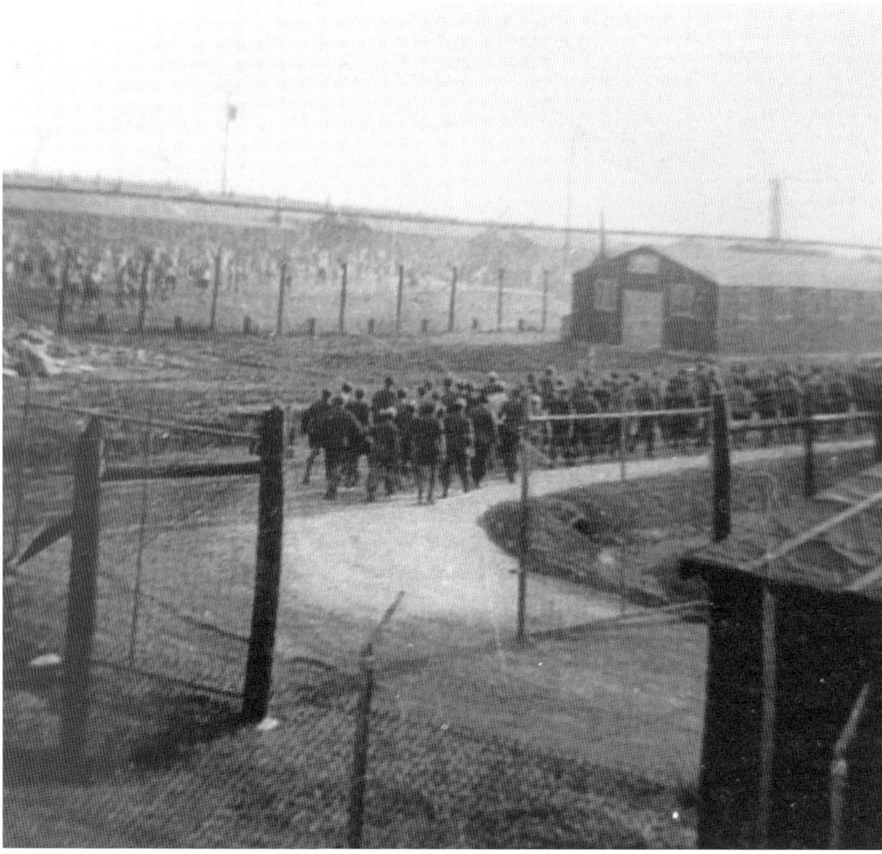

German prisoners of war. *Courtesy of the Fort Reno Museum.*

you step through the entryway. Wood laid floors are seen throughout the upstairs sanctuary, with solid carved wooden benches lining each side of the aisle. Cross timbers support the high arched ceiling, with wooden carved chandeliers adorning the hall. A wooden pulpit sits below the curved archway outlining the stage, and a wooden hand-carved cross adorns the wall directly behind it. Arched glass windows line the walls, allowing the sun to cast eerie shadows across the floor. At the front of the sanctuary, to the west of the pulpit is an open doorway that leads to an office located just behind the stage as well as to a narrow staircase that leads down into the basement area of the building. Short ceilings and steel round beams support the sanctuary above. In the basement area, you will find a small kitchen, as well as an open area to set up tables for a wedding or event.

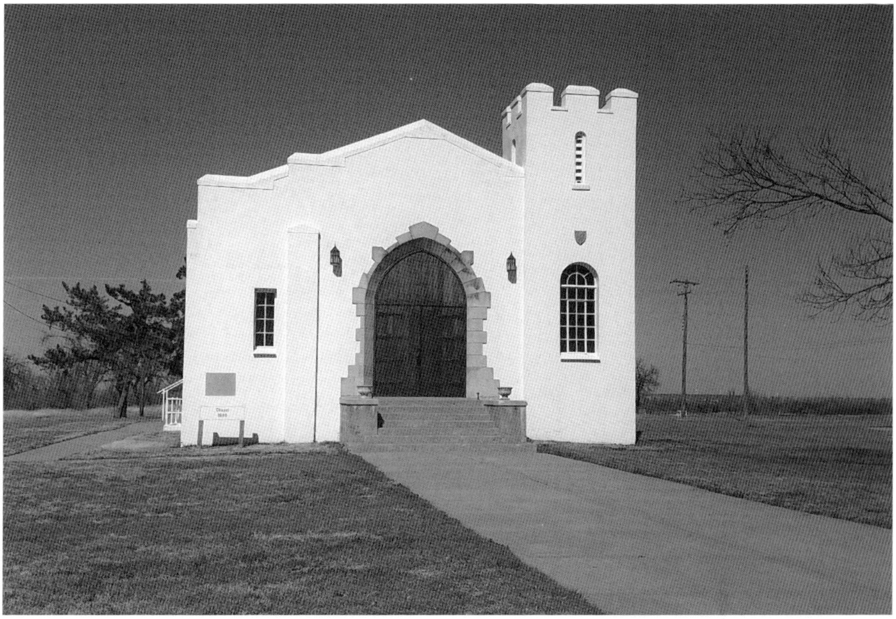

Fort Reno chapel. *Courtesy of Tanya McCoy.*

Several years ago, fascinated with some of the history as well as the paranormal stories associated with the site, I decided to hold one of our paranormal conferences at the old chapel. It was a weekend filled with great speakers, investigations, vendors and a psychic gallery reading. As usual, things did not always go as planned, but everything ended up working out, and before we knew it, the event was over. After the guests had left and the vendors had packed up and gone, I found myself alone in the basement of the building doing some last-minute cleaning when I heard what sounded like someone walking around upstairs. Being responsible for the site, I quickly went upstairs to see who was still in the building. The front doors remained locked, and the only way to exit would be to take the only set of stairs down into the basement—the exact ones I had just come up. No one had passed me on the stairs. With the stairs being so narrow, it would be hard for someone to do it at all. I took a quick turn around the upstairs, looking down all the aisle seats, the changing room and the office. No one was in the building with me—well, at least not anyone living. I definitely did not feel as if I were alone. I descended the stairs back into the basement only to ascend the outside staircase to meet the rest of my group at the car. I told them about what I had just experienced. My car was parked next to the basement door. No one had been seen entering or leaving the building but me. I know what I heard that day; the heavy footsteps of an unseen presence could be heard plainly echoing throughout the building. I have no explanation for where they came from, but I do know that something or someone was there with me that day. Could it be one of the prisoners who helped to build the chapel so many years ago? Does the wood and mortar hold their energy from the past as they skillfully carved the edges into the wood? The old chapel holds a special feeling all its own, just waiting for you to pass through the archway of its wooden doors.

THE VICTORIAN HOUSE AT FORT RENO

On the northeast corner of the Fort Reno grounds sits an old Victorian house. The three-story home was built in 1889 for the daughter of a wealthy man who was unhappy with living the tent life at the fort. It is said she would write home to her father complaining about how miserable her living conditions were. She was used to the finer things in life, and being the wife of an officer in the military did have its drawbacks. Soon, her father shipped all the goods necessary to build his little girl a better place to call home. Only the best building materials were used in the construction of the home, and it is one of the few buildings left standing today. The home had fallen into some disrepair over the decades, but thanks to a special group of people helping to preserve history, this glorious home has been restored for many more generations to come.

The house is large, with several large rooms on the first level. Just inside the front door is the staircase leading up to the second floor, and an old brick fireplace can be seen as you peer through the time-worn glass lining the windows. This home is not open to tours. Guests can, however, walk around the white painted porch and peer into several windows to catch a glimpse of what the house looks like today. One can only imagine the dinner parties and afternoon teas that must have taken place here so many years ago.

The Victorian house has been considered one of the most haunted locations at Fort Reno even though it is not open to public investigations. Ron Cross shared some of his experiences he had while leading ghost tours at Fort Reno many years ago. It was around 2006–07 when Ron first contacted the historical society at the fort. He had heard that they were doing ghost tours, so he and his group volunteered to assist with them. While helping

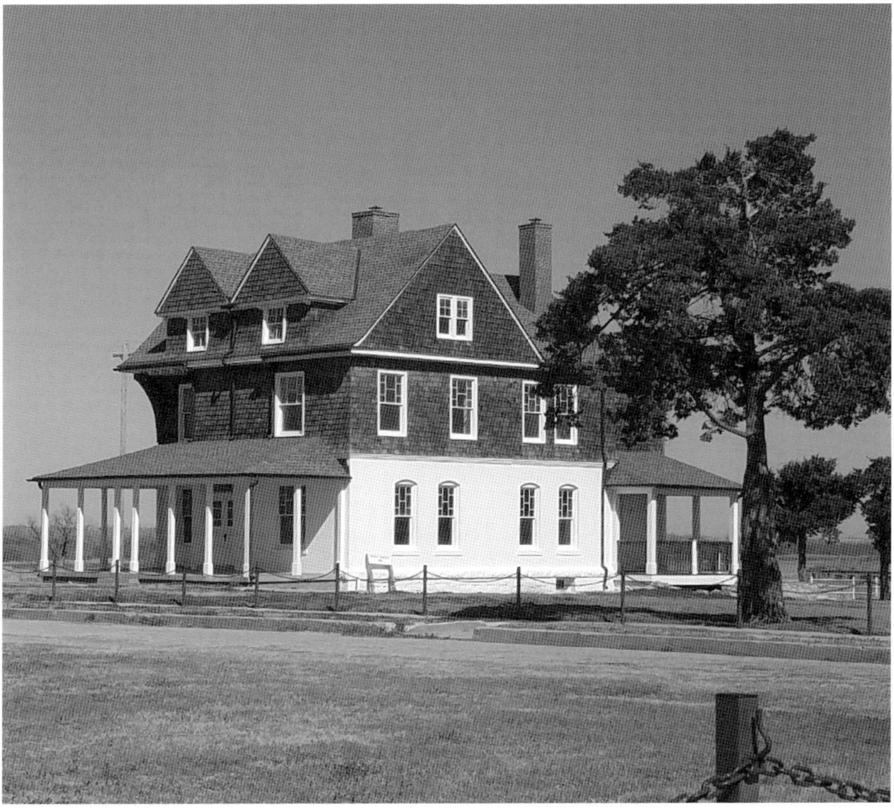

Old Victorian home at Fort Reno. *Courtesy of Tanya McCoy.*

with the tours, his group was able to investigate inside the home. He recalled an incident they witnessed one night while investigating. He and one of his team members were standing about twelve feet away from the stairs talking while some other members were upstairs investigating another part of the home. Jessica was talking to Ron when he looked over toward the staircase, and there stood a full-body apparition of a woman in a long white dress. He stared at her in disbelief for several moments, and then the woman simply disappeared. As he was turning toward Jessica to see if she had seen the woman standing on the staircase, another member came down the stairs and asked if they had been standing on the staircase just then. It seems they, too, had seen the mysterious lady in white.

Another spirit that appears around the house is that of a little girl. She doesn't show herself to just anyone; she only likes to let her presence be known to other children. There have been several reports over the years of parents seeing their children waving at something up in one of the second-floor windows. When asked what they are waving at, the children always reply, "The little girl who is waving at me." Children have also reported seeing her playing around the house in the yard, as well as on the porch.

Another presence has also been felt in the home, that of a male. Many people have reported feeling as if there is a man standing behind or near them, but no one has ever reported seeing him. The basement of the house also has strange occurrences. It is reported that a strong cigarette smell will appear out of nowhere. Ron's team had an experience in the basement. While doing an investigation, a strong smell of cigarette smoke filled the air. Ron went outside to look around the house to see if anyone was smoking, but no one was there.

Ron also experienced another paranormal event at the Victorian home, or rather directly outside. It was a windy night (seeing as it's Oklahoma, that should come as no surprise), and the building directly across from the home had a screen door that was not closed properly. The door began to bang in the wind, causing a lot of noise contamination, so one of the team members said she was going to go close the door more securely. Ron told her he would run across and do it instead, not wanting her to go out by herself. It had been raining outside, so he grabbed his umbrella and headed toward the other building. There was a tall tree between the two buildings, and he felt something pulling on his umbrella. He thought he had perhaps snagged it on one of the tree limbs, but as he turned around, he noticed the tree limbs were too high to even touch his umbrella. He could continue to feel the tug of the umbrella, but due to the direction it was being pulled toward, he knew it couldn't have been the wind doing it. As he turned to proceed toward the building, he looked down and noticed three skunks directly in his path. Had he not had to stop due to the pulling on his umbrella, he would have walked directly into their path. Was the spirit trying to warn him of the impending danger? Lucky for him, the spirit was in the right place at the right time.

Another incident happened to a group of visitors who had been visiting the fort. A group of young teens was standing in front of the house a few yards away having their picture taken with the Victorian house directly behind them. Later, when they were looking over the photos, they noticed a woman standing on the porch in the background. They sent the picture to the Fort Reno museum, and I was lucky enough to see it. It was as the

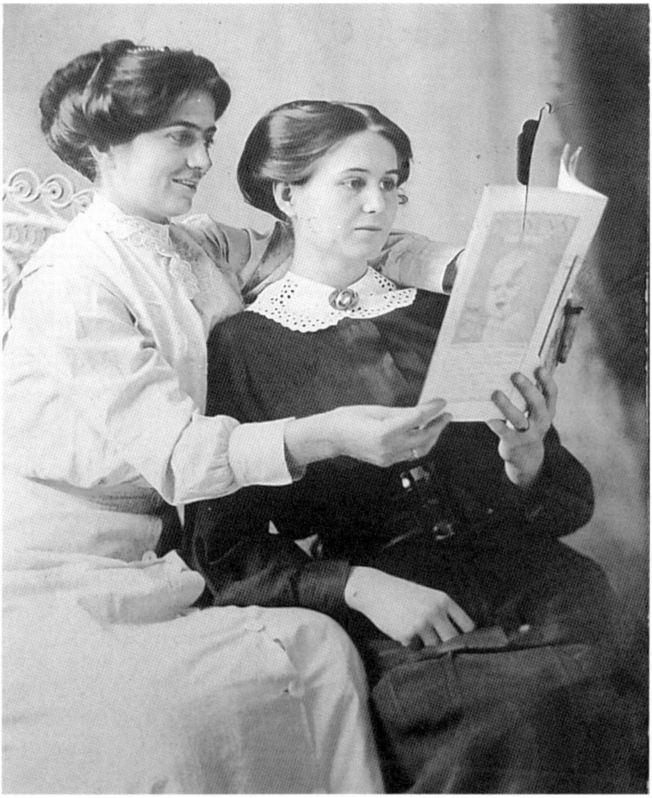

Victorian women at Fort Reno. *Courtesy of the Fort Reno Museum.*

girls had said: standing directly behind them was a full-body apparition of a woman in a long dress reaching to the ground. Her hair was up in what appeared to be a bun style, and she was standing with her hands on her hips, facing out to where the girls were standing. The girls claimed that no one else was there when the picture was taken, and in my personal option the woman appeared to be wearing period clothing. Could this possibly be the woman in the long dress that so many people have witnessed over the years, and if so, why does she choose to stay at the home? Did something horrific happen here, or did she love her home so much that she simply chose not to leave? If you find yourself visiting Fort Reno, make sure you stop and take a look at the old Victorian house. Maybe you will be lucky enough to see the woman of the house. Just be careful to watch your step; you don't want to run into any skunks while you're there.

FORT RENO CEMETERY

A short drive along a gravel road, just west of the fort, sits a waist-high wall of stone that surrounds the Fort Reno Cemetery. The cemetery is the final resting place for military personnel and their family members, civilian employees and their families and prisoners of war from World War II. Of the nearly two hundred graves, approximately one-third are those of soldiers, most of whom did not die in battle.

Traditional opinion implies that all cemeteries are creepy or eerie places. I find that most are quite peaceful places of rest. I had visited the cemetery before, sometime during high school, and remember it being my favorite part of the fort; I've always been a fan of older grave markers. As I walked up to the modest gate with a small sign reading "Fort Reno Cemetery," this time was different. The difference may have been that I actually knew some of the history of the fort and its function, and let's face it, history is a little more appreciated with age. It was a windy day, not surprising for the plains. I almost did not want to open the guest book to sign for fear of pages being ripped away; however, I'm glad I did. Visitors from all over, even overseas, had come here to pay their respects. Coins dot the gravestones throughout the cemetery, placed there by men and women who have also served in the military. It is serene.

I wondered who the lady in white that has been reported to be seen tucked between the cedar trees might be. Is she buried here? Had she been visiting a loved one who was buried here? Did she work here at the fort? Could she

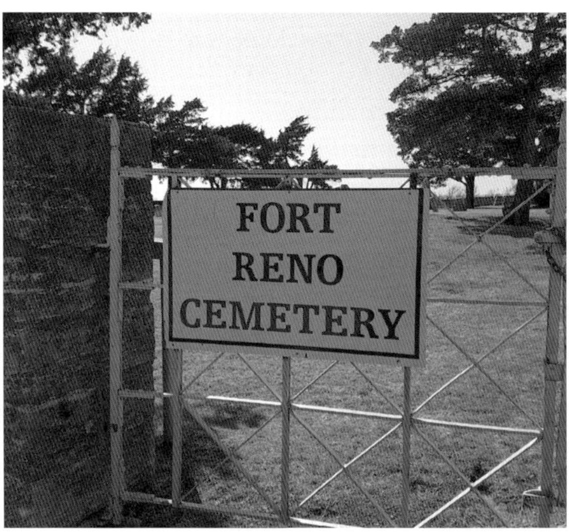

Fort Reno Cemetery. *Courtesy of Tanya McCoy.*

be the wife of the notable Indian scout Benjamin Clark, who is also interred at the fort's cemetery?

Benjamin Clark started his military career at the young age of thirteen as a post courier at Fort Bridger, Wyoming. He served in the Sixth Kansas Cavalry during the Civil War, patrolling the Arkansas and Missouri borders. Following the Civil War, Clark managed pack trains and married his first wife, a Cheyenne woman known as Emily, and had his first child, a girl named Jennie. Emily died in January 1873. Clark remarried following the death of his first wife, this time to a Cheyenne woman named Red Fern, with whom he had another child, named Emily. Ben's second wife died in 1880, and he remarried later the same year, to a woman named Moka, also known as "Little Woman." Ben Clark and Moka had twelve children, five of whom died before 1900. Clark became fluent in the Cheyenne and Arapaho languages and was respected by Indians and whites alike. He joined as an army scout in 1868. He served as chief of scouts for General Philip Sheridan and Lieutenant Colonel George Custer. Moka died on May 6, 1913. After many years of service, the loss of his third wife and suffering from paralysis, Benjamin Clark ended his own life in his quarters on Fort Reno. That building is still standing today but is not open to the public. It is termed by staff the Ben Clark House. Benjamin Clark and his wife are buried in the fort's cemetery. Several people have reported a feeling of being choked when around the house.

Near the outside of the cemetery, a member of a paranormal team leading ghost tours of the fort recorded an EVP of someone saying, "I know, I know, I was run over." Upon searching through records, it was found that Tim O'Connell, an employee of the quartermaster department, was helping three soldiers move to the fort on January 1, 1899. While O'Connell was riding one of the mules, one of the soldiers hopped on the back of the mule, startling the animal and throwing both riders. O'Connell landed in front of the wagon and was killed almost instantly when the wagon ran over him. He is buried in the fort's cemetery with a tombstone that simply reads "O'Connell."

Perhaps the most somber part of the cemetery, aside from the many graves of children, is the western section. This section is the final resting place of 70 prisoners of war. During World War II, 1,300 POWs were brought to Fort Reno. Many of these POWs were from General Erwin Rommel's Afrika Korps and had been captured in North Africa. Many of the prisoners were hired as laborers at the fort and local farms. Prisoners built the chapel, which is still standing and open for tours today, in 1944. Of the 70 POWs buried

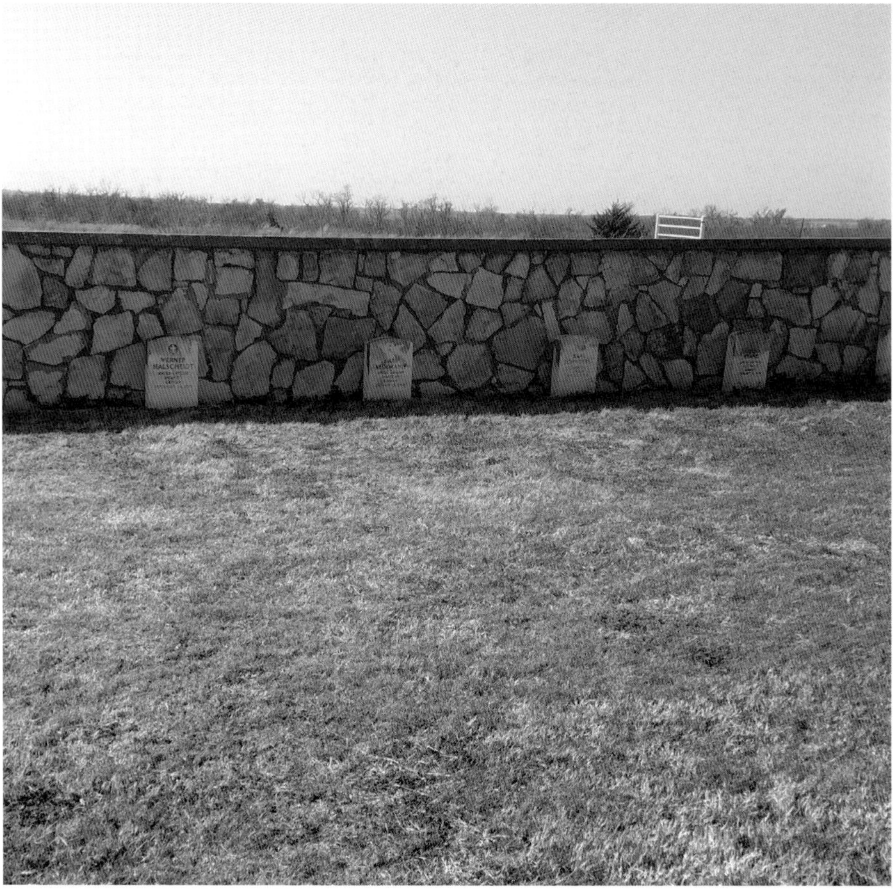

POW graves at Fort Reno. *Courtesy of Tanya McCoy.*

here, only one actually died on the fort; most died in military camps around Oklahoma and Texas and were brought to the fort cemetery for burial.

Sightings of a male full-body apparition have been reported in the old commissary/armory building, which is not currently open to the public. Patrons and staff have reported seeing the same thing at different times of the day. Several people have seen a young man asking, "Is this a joke?" On April 24, 1885, William Stockwell, who had not been feeling well, sought out the drug quinine. The only other personnel in the vicinity directed him to a bottle sitting on the windowsill. William questioned the substance inside but took a large dose after being assured by several other comrades that the contents of the bottle were, indeed, quinine. Stockwell lived for two hours

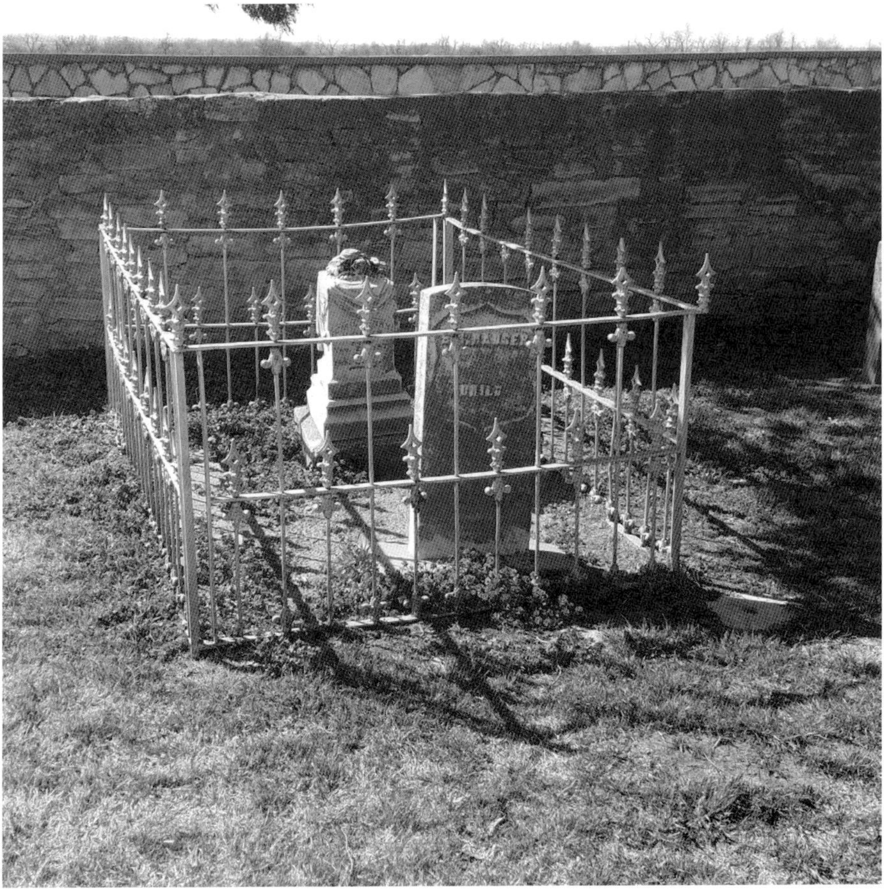

Fort Reno grave. *Courtesy of Tanya McCoy.*

after taking this fatal dose. It was later confirmed by the doctor that the contents of that bottle were, in fact, strychnine. William was twenty-five years old when he died, and he is buried at the fort.

The number of children buried here (fifty-six) is telling of the mortality rate for infants and children during the time that the fort was functioning. Perhaps the lady in white seen tucked between the trees still watches over them.

THE CANADIAN COUNTY HISTORICAL MUSEUM

Located near the heart of El Reno at 300 South Grand Avenue sits the Canadian County Historical Museum. Tucked away from any major highway or roads, the buildings of El Reno's past, once separated miles apart, now sit closer to one another to give you a small glimpse into this city's historical past.

The museum was chartered in October 1968 and opened its doors to the public in 1970. Jack and Patricia Reuter spent most of their life collecting relics, including most of what you will see in the museum today. From Native American goods and art to an old bar top with a large mirror used during the original land run, the museum has plenty to offer anyone wishing to learn a little more about Oklahoma and its history.

The museum sits on a corner lot that extends from the street up to the railroad tracks. There are eight historic buildings on the property, including the original Rock Island Railroad depot. Built in 1907, the Rock Island Railroad connected El Reno to all points of the United States. During World War I, soldiers traveling through the United States would often stop at the depot to purchase paper goods and other supplies from the Red Cross canteen prior to leaving overseas. The original building, built by a local

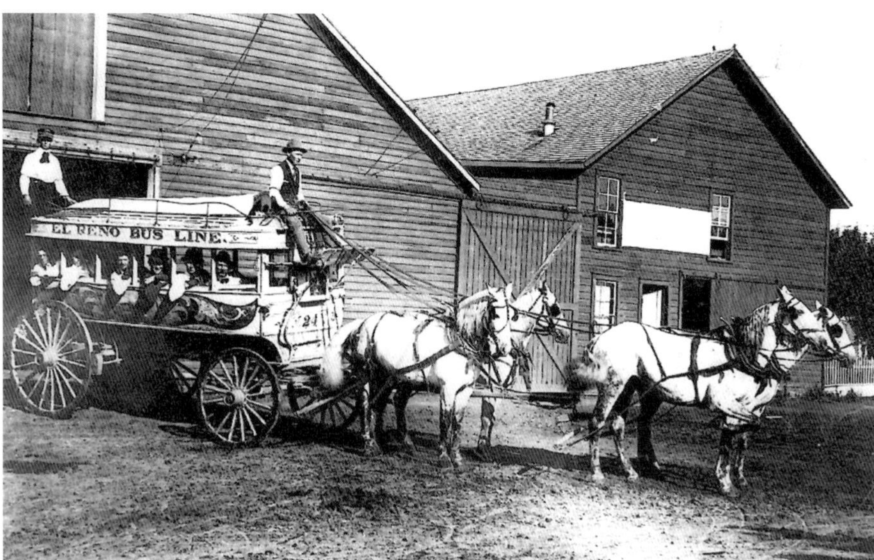

Historic Fort Reno. *Courtesy of Tanya McCoy.*

group of Boy Scouts, can still be seen today and is located on-site. The inside of the building is closed due to disrepair.

The Rock Island Depot had its dark days in the past. During the segregation period, African Americans were not allowed in the same area of the building as white people. They had their own drinking area and waiting area. While the whites had nice benches to sit on and wait for the train to arrive, the African Americans were left to wait in the baggage claim area, where the luggage and various goods would be unloaded off the train. Today, that area holds memories and collections of the railroad's past, as well as a few ghostly remains of years gone by.

As you walk from the baggage claim area toward the main ticketing area, you pass through a walkway filled with historical pictures and cameras. Old family photos line the walls, and family photo albums dating back to the 1800s are stored behind two glass showcases. There are several types of cameras on display for anyone with a passion for photography. Cameras used over one hundred years ago can be found behind these glass cases for everyone to enjoy. From family photos to single portraits, the eyes of yesteryear follow you as you move into the next rooms of the museum.

The next room you enter is filled with the history of local doctors, along with their various equipment and supplies. From old glass medicine bottles

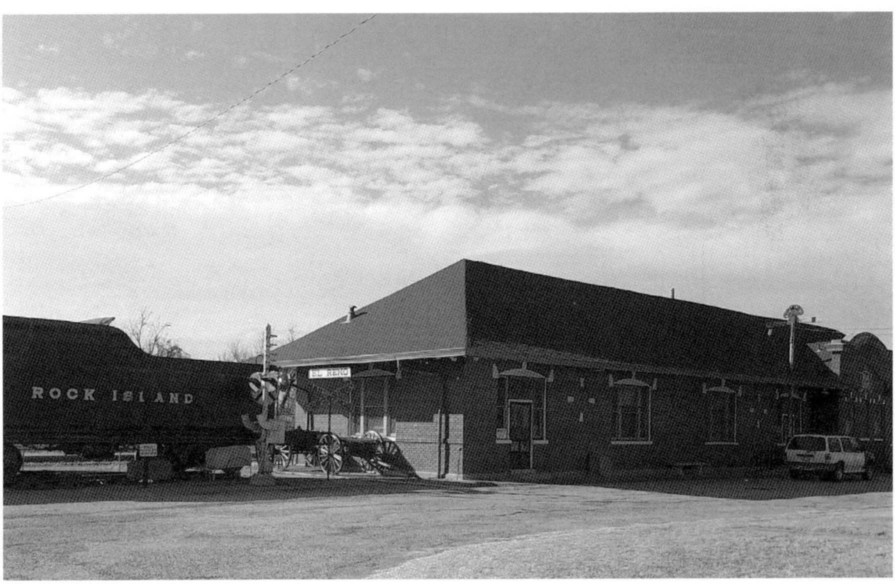

Canadian County Museum. *Courtesy of Tanya McCoy.*

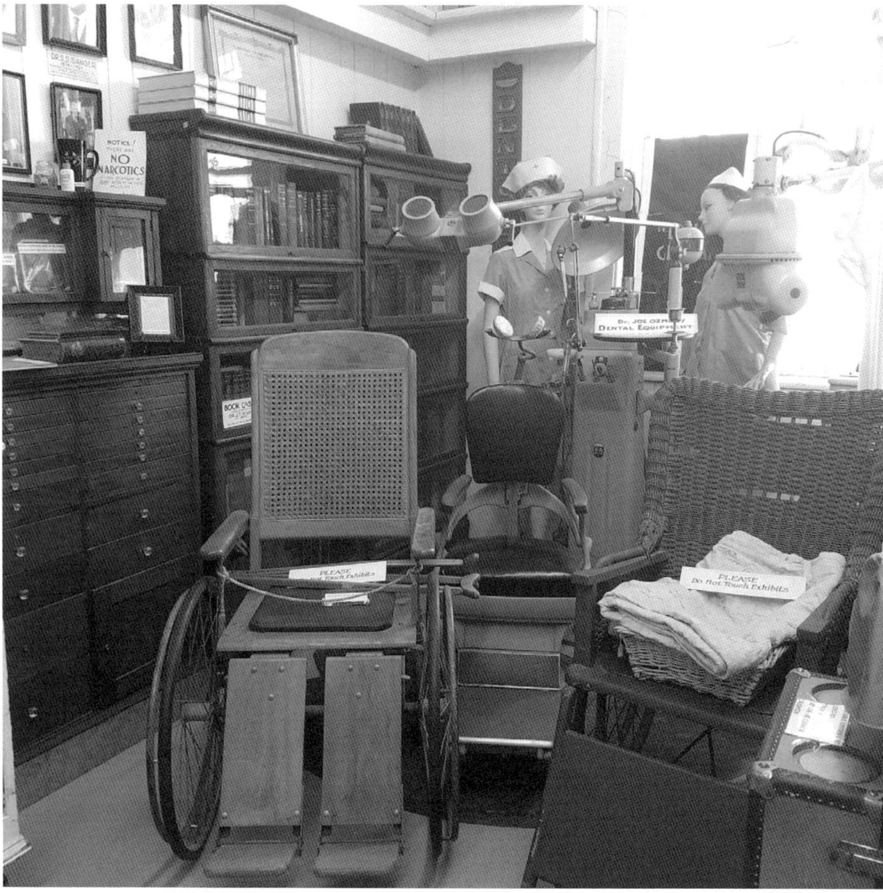

Various medical equipment at the Canadian County Museum. *Courtesy of Tanya McCoy.*

to a nurse's uniform, this room has just about everything to showcase the old frontier's medical treatments in the everyday life of a doctor. Bone saws lie in glass cases along with syringes (the non-disposable, reusable and no-safety-cap kind), medicine bags, personal clothing and a doctor's exam table. There is even an old child-size, reusable burial suit on display as well. If that's not creepy enough for you, just move over to the next glass case, where you can see hundreds of human teeth lying about.

Dr. Jonas B. Spitler is one of the early day physicians featured at the museum. He was considered the first physician to practice in the Oklahoma and Indian Territories. Arriving prior to statehood, Dr. Spitler first arrived on horseback. Soon, he was making his rounds in a buggy, and he went

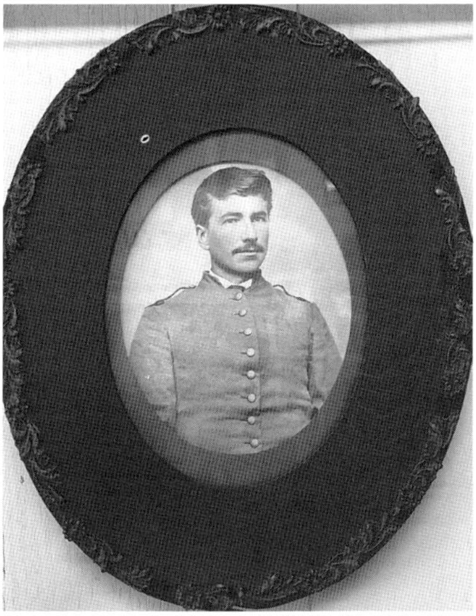

Dr. Joseph Spitler, first doctor in Mustang. *Courtesy of the Canadian County Museum.*

on to settle in the Mustang area. Dr. Spitler graduated from the University of Illinois and went on to attend Keokuk Medical School in Iowa. In 1892, he and his family moved into the Oklahoma Territory. Dr. Spitler was a true physician, giving his heart and soul to helping people. Doctors back then didn't make a lot of money and often faced financial difficulties just like their neighbors. Not only would he never refuse care to anyone, despite their ability to pay, but he would also often cross the Canadian River to spend days tending to the sick Indians of the Chickasaw Nation. He is considered one of the founding fathers of Mustang, Oklahoma.

As we continue through the building, we pass the old ticket seller's booth, the original window still intact, as if it were open and ready to sell tickets to the awaiting customers. This area leads out into a larger open area, which was originally the waiting area for the depot. Solid wood benches, still sturdy and in place, are located to the front of the building. Along its walls you will find various artifacts, many from the local Indian tribes of Oklahoma. Ceremonial dress, headdresses, weapons, a buffalo head and many other items are showcased to help a person understand a little more about the American Indians' way of life prior to statehood.

Frontier life was no easy task. Many people perished, while many others thrived and continued to build homes for themselves and their families on the Oklahoma plains. The museum showcases various items from Oklahoma's earliest days, from hat pins to shoes, clothing and even furniture; you can truly get a sense of what life may have been like over a century ago.

The first time I investigated the building was around 2013. We set up several cameras around the building and gathered our equipment. Our first destination was the main lobby area. As we sat quietly in the darkness, we could hear the wooden floor planks creaking as the old building began to settle. We strained our eyes against the darkness to see if we could detect any movement or possibly see any shadows. We started our EVP session asking general questions: "Is anyone here with us tonight that would like to speak with us?" The silence continued. After about thirty minutes with no activity occurring, we decided we would move back to the baggage area to try our luck there. We continued the investigation by asking general questions once more and by conducting a K2 (an EMF device used to pick up on electromagnetic fields or energy fields) sweep of the area. Since there were very few windows in the rooms, we decided we would use the FLIR (a thermal imaging camera used to pick up on temperature changes in the area), doing our best to avoid the glass in the showcases. As we were panning around the room, we noticed a change in one area. A picture was quickly snapped on the camera. We were soon getting responses to our questions on our voice box device. When we reviewed the picture and our audio, we discovered that we had been visiting with an elderly African American man. We never did discover how he was or why he had chosen to stay there after he had passed away. Was he attached to an object in the room, or was he perhaps an old railroad employee who was simply happy being around the things he knew best? Perhaps on future investigations we might be able to unlock the mystery of the man if he still resides at the old train depot.

Just across the drive, a few yards away, sits one of El Reno's oldest hotels, the Hotel El Reno. Built in 1892 by J.M. Kemp, it is the oldest standing commercial building in El Reno.

The hotel once stood at the corner of Choctaw and Wade and was in use until 1975, when it closed its doors. The building was later donated to the museum and moved to the site in 1984. It is an old two-story, wood-framed building, created in a Folk Victorian style. The museum has restored it as close as possible to its original appearance. When you first step into the building, you are welcomed by a small living room area filled with antique chairs, an old fireplace and the check-in desk with the old cubbies and room keys still visible. After you "check into" the hotel, you can ascend the narrow, steep staircase to go up to your room—just be careful not to bump your head on the low-level ceiling. People seem to have been much shorter back in those days. Once upstairs, you are met with a group of small doors lining each wall. The wooden doors that once provided privacy have since been replaced by glass windows, giving you a peek into the past of what this hotel would have looked like. You will not find a soft king-sized bed here but, rather, a small cast-iron frame bed with an old hand-sewn quilt to keep you warm on those cold winter nights. A public bathroom was often shared between all the guests, whether it be an indoor or outdoor restroom, depending on the time in history. Downstairs, guests would take their meals in a small dining room with a small kitchen adjacent to it, making it easier

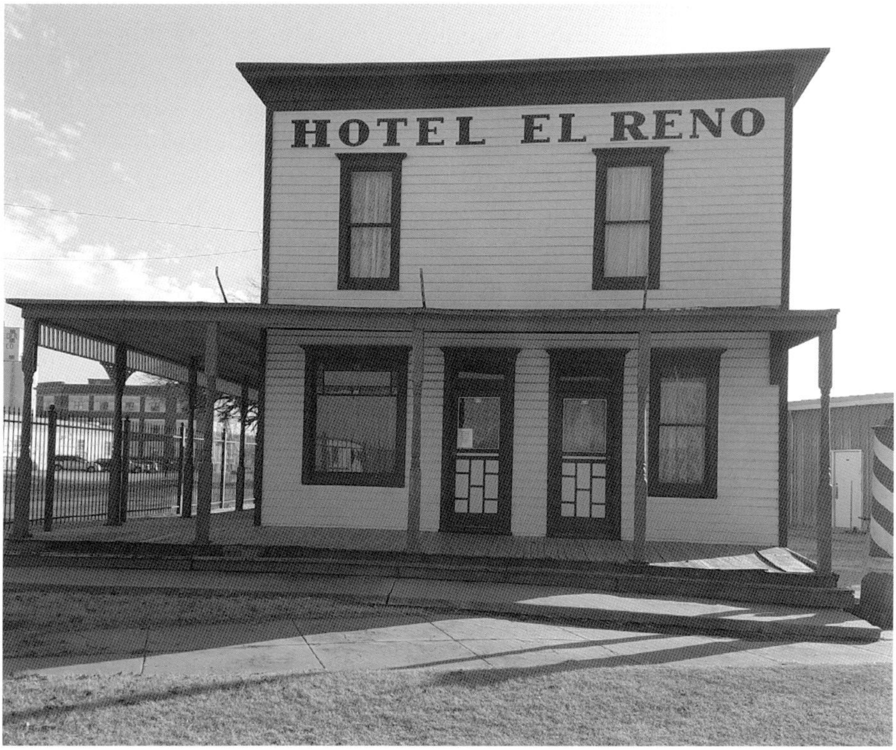

Hotel El Reno, the first hotel in El Reno, Oklahoma. *Courtesy of Tanya McCoy.*

for staff to serve the food. It was in the dining room area that we decided to set up our DVR system.

With several reports of people hearing footsteps and even running being heard, we set up our audio equipment throughout the hotel. The building is small and easily accessible, so we decided we would only run four of our night-vision cameras throughout the building. We placed two upstairs, one facing in each direction, and two downstairs, one facing into the dining room and the other facing out into the open common room or front lobby. Since we were a small team that night, we all decided to stay together to help decrease the chances of cross-contamination of noise. We started our first EVP session in the dining room of the old hotel. We were almost an hour into the investigation, and nothing much had happened so far (which can be very common on a true investigation; it's not like the overdramatized TV shows). It was a very quiet evening, and despite it being Oklahoma, there was little to no wind at all that night. As we were sitting quietly downstairs, we all heard a very distinct *thump* coming from right above our heads. We quickly turned to one another to see if we all had heard the noise. Soon after, another loud noise was heard. Then, much to our surprise, the thumping increased, getting louder and louder, then faster and faster. Before long, it sounded as if someone or something was running back and forth down the small hallway upstairs. Two of us jumped up and started toward the staircase. We could still hear the running as we approached the stairs. Just as we grabbed the stair rail to ascend, the noise stopped. When we reached the top of the stairs, no one was in sight. There was a distinct chill in the air despite it being summertime and very warm outside. We knew we were not alone. There was no sign of any animal being present, nor could a living person have been up there to make the noise. There is only one way up and one way down, and from where we were sitting, no one could have ascended the stairs without us knowing. When we pulled the footage from our camera system, you could plainly make out what appeared to be a mist forming in the middle of the hall. It was small in stature, no more than four feet tall, and you could see it moving around in the hallway. You could also see as it started to dissipate just prior to our arrival. Was this a friendly spirit simply playing a game of hide-and-seek, or did we perhaps scare off whatever may have been running around upstairs when we decided to search out the noises heard from below? We didn't experience much after that, and the building seemed to quiet down. Hopefully one day we will be able to find out more about the ghostly footsteps of the historic El Reno hotel.

There are various other buildings located around the property of the museum, but one location does not consist of wooden walls or brick and mortar. Sitting beside the old railroad tracks between the depot and the big red barn is an old caboose car. You will not find a GPS system or even an old radio here. Years ago, travel was much different than today. If you were lucky enough to afford the finer things in life, then you might be able to purchase a ticket on the train. It was a much easier way to travel, and it would decrease your chances of getting saddle sore. Once you purchased your ticket on the train, you could sit back and relax as you watched the beauty of the landscape pass by just outside your window—that is, if the loud rumbling of the steel wheels on the track and the blowing of the whistle didn't bother you too much. The vibrations of the turning of the wheels and the swaying of the train car made for a long trip across open country, often riding days on end to reach your destination. The old caboose is where employees of the railroad would sleep on long trips.

Fitted with a few small bunks and pull-down seats, this small space was often home to the railroad workers.

These days, the car is accessible for you to walk in and look around, but some of the activity takes place just outside it. We didn't get to investigate the old caboose due to our time, but we did get to witness something. As we stood facing the train, several of us saw what appeared to be legs walking back and forth behind the train car. It wasn't just one set of legs but two. We walked around the other side to see if there was anyone else inside the museum grounds with us that night. With it being after-hours, no one should have been on the property but us at that time. When we walked behind it, no one was there. Just beyond the cars is a chain-link fence, and past it is the railroad. No one was around, and if they had been, there was nowhere they could have run without us seeing them. We are not sure who was walking around the old train caboose that night, but what we do know for certain is that it wasn't someone who was still alive.

Also located on the property is an old church, the old Menneville Mennonite Church. The building houses several pews, a pulpit and an old piano. The pulpit still stands, waiting for the pastor to preach out to his onward-looking congregation. Next to the church sits an old one-room schoolhouse with a potbelly stove, teacher's desk and several old students'

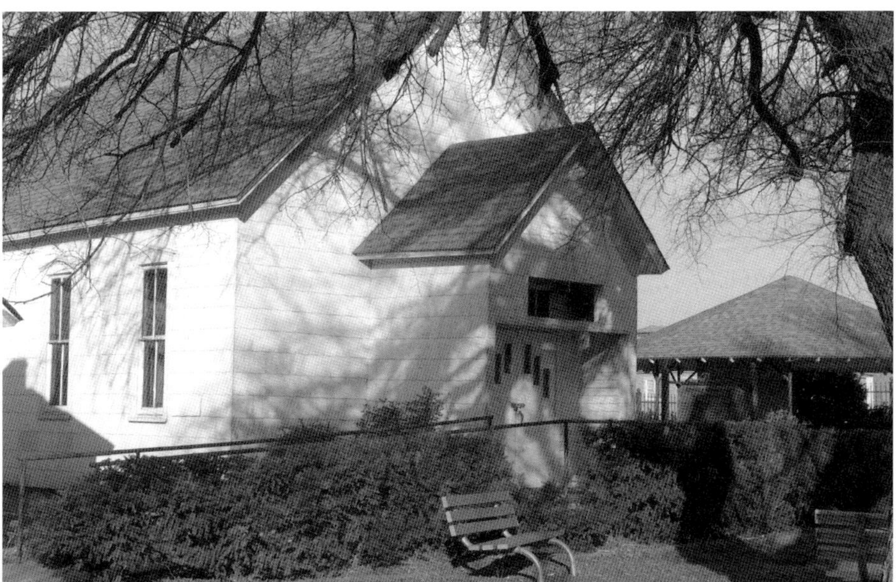

Old church at the Canadian County Museum. *Courtesy of Tanya McCoy.*

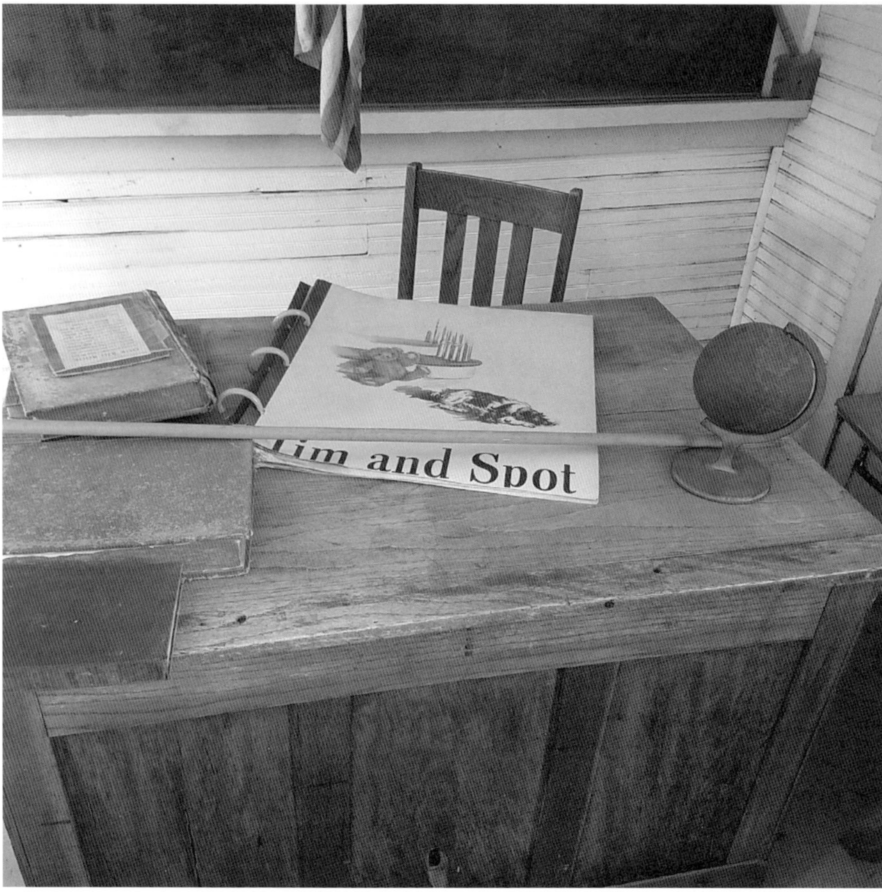

Old one-room school at the Canadian County Museum. *Courtesy of Tanya McCoy.*

desks in two small rows. The large red barn sits next to the old hotel and is filled with various items, including carriages, pictures, various articles of clothing, old trunks and, my personal favorite, a solid wood bar with the original old time-warped mirror used in the original Oklahoma land run. A few feet behind the barn sits the original Darling jailhouse, a small building housing two small cells. Its iron bars are still in place. American Indians who didn't follow the strict rules or refused to forget their native ways were often housed here. It is also said that the Doolin gang—an American outlaw gang also known as the Wild Bunch, known for robbing stagecoaches, trains and banks across Oklahoma as well as Arkansas and Kansas during the 1890s—spent some time in this small jailhouse. Just behind the jail sits General

Sheridan's headquarters. This small log building was once located at Fort Reno and was later moved to the property to become part of the museum. With all this Oklahoma history located in one small area, how could such a place not be haunted? Whether you are interested in local history or the paranormal, the Canadian County Historical Museum is a must-see for any traveler and well worth a trip.

ELKS LODGE #743

The Benevolent and Protective Order of Elks was started as a social club in New York City in 1868 by Charles Vivian. The Elks lodge hosted social gatherings and performances for its members, and membership grew quickly, leading to requests for lodges in other cities. Vivian's vision for the Elks was a charitable one. Among some of the Elks' contributions have been setting up field hospitals during World War I, providing loans/scholarships for veterans returning from war, donating more than half a million pints of blood during the Korean War and volunteering to write letters to soldiers during Operation Desert Storm. Of course, this isn't an exhaustive list. The tradition of charitable giving carries on in individual lodges. From helping members in distress to funding scholarships for high school students, the Elks have a mission to make their communities better places.

The Elks lodge in El Reno is a beautiful three-story building with a dry basement. It was built in 1904 at the St. Louis World's Fair as a headquarters for the Oklahoma Territory to promote statehood. In 1905, the building was split up and brought to El Reno on the Rock Island Railroad and was reassembled in its resting place on Rock Island Avenue. The façade of the building was remodeled in the 1970s and remains the same to this day.

As you enter the lodge on the main level, you are greeted by a large open ballroom area. Wooden floors line the hall, and tall white columns extend from the floor to the ceiling. To the back of the hall is a kitchen area stocked with various dishes and glasses ready to be used for the next big event. Many people have reported hearing the dishes clanking and glasses being moved when no one was present. To the front of the hall is a small stage area. As I sat on the stairs looking out onto the dance floor, I could see soldiers dressed in their uniforms as they took the arms of young ladies and led them onto the dance floor. I could almost hear the band playing an upbeat tune as I looked out into a sea of young couples enjoying the night. It was like

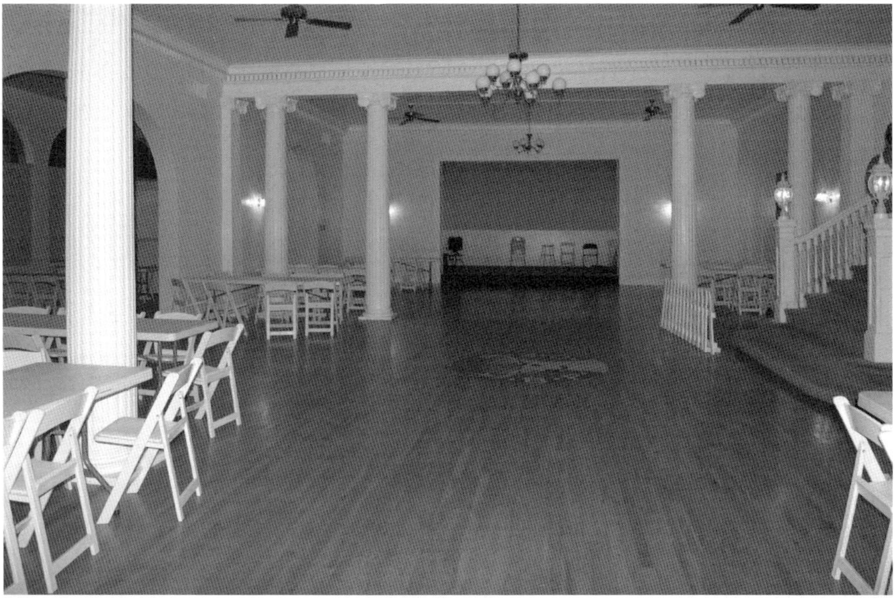

Elks ballroom. *Courtesy of Tanya McCoy.*

watching a movie playing out in front of my very own eyes. Later, when I told our host what I had seen while sitting in the ballroom, she informed me that I was not the only person to have witnessed that, as others have also seen or felt the same thing in that area.

A large wide staircase leads up to the next floor. A beautiful stained-glass window can be seen adorning the wall. As you ascend the staircase, you come to a landing area. From there, a set of stairs lines both walls, leading you farther up onto the next level. The staircase to the right leads to an open room with a small bar area. Wood paneling and mirrors line one of the walls, and if you look closely, you might just see the entrance to a small wooden room. This secret room holds various items, from an old pool table to broken crystal chandeliers. What other secrets the walls might hold is unknown to us. On one of the walls in the room, there is a picture of one of the Elks' past members. No matter how many times workers straighten the picture, it always tends to move. People have also reported feeling uncomfortable, like the man in the picture is staring at them. When we first walked up to the third level with our dear friend and host for the night, Cortney Kane Sides, we had all been standing around talking when I caught a movement out of the corner of my eye. I turned to look at the staircase that led up to that

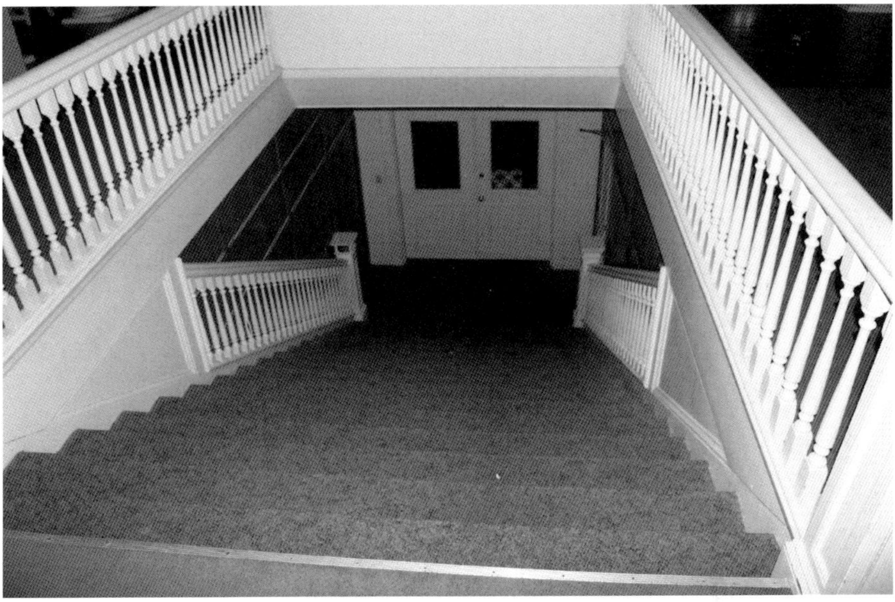

Elks staircase. *Courtesy of Tanya McCoy.*

room and saw a middle-aged man walk up the stairs and then turn and walk into the room we had just come out of. I asked Cortney if anyone else was in the building, and she answered no. I told her what I had just seen, so we walked over to the room and looked in, but there was no one there.

We returned to the other side as we continued with our tour. On the opposite side of the building was another set of rooms: one large room with a padlock on it and a few smaller ones opposite that. The smaller ones were mainly used for storage, but the larger room was more interesting. It was the meeting room for the order of the Elks and closed to the public, leaving an air of mystery surrounding it.

In the lower level of the building you will find three primary areas: the open foyer, the game room and the bar. The open foyer sits between the game room and the bar. There is a large round table there with several chairs around it for people to sit and visit or perhaps play a round of cards. The game room plays host to several pool tables, a jukebox and various other games. In this area there is another kitchen area that serves the bar area. Cortney confided in us that she herself didn't feel very comfortable in that area and tries to avoid it whenever possible. There is a set of restrooms adjacent to the game room. Many people report a feeling of uneasiness in the women's bathroom; some even refuse to look in the mirror out of fear of seeing someone or something else standing there. Many have reported feeling dizzy when they first walk into the area, almost causing them to feel disoriented.

On the opposite side of the building is a small bar area. The room has several small tables with chairs set up around the room and a large bar area to the back. Someone was in the bar area by himself when he heard noises coming from behind the bar area. Shot glasses flying off the shelves have also been reported. Doors and chairs have been known to move on their own, as if being pushed by unseen hands.

Various other stories have been reported as well. From missing objects to growls being heard, the Elks lodge appears to play host to several different types of hauntings. Despite whatever restless spirit haunts the Elks lodge, the building remains a beautiful facility to host any event; just make sure you set an extra table setting for any unseen guest who might wish to join the party.

THE CENTRE THEATRE

The Centre Theatre in El Reno, Oklahoma, first opened its doors on December 1, 1944. Built on one of the main streets in the downtown area, the Centre offered its patrons an exciting experience in the world of drama and comedy direct from movies featuring some of Hollywood's A list. From Humphrey Bogart's "Here's looking at you, kid," to Katharine Hepburn's "Oh, that's silly. No woman would ever run for president. She'd have to admit she's over thirty-five," the theater brought a little bit of joy and romance into each viewer's life.

The Centre was constructed in an early Art Deco style, featuring a small lobby with a concession area ready to greet everyone who showed up to enjoy an ice-cold Coke and popcorn. Guests would be greeted by the ushers as they entered the main auditorium of the theater. With almost seven hundred seats to choose from, they could have their choice of seating. To the front of the theater is a medium-size wooden stage with a large movie screen stretching down from the ceiling. Blue-covered cushioned seats stretch from the floor up several sets of stairs to the old projection booth. It's in the projection area that our story begins.

When we first arrived at the theater, it appeared very small in size. When I went to the theater to gather some more information about its history, I was reminded just how big the theater is. Cara, one of my team members, and I met Heather Brothers, an employee of the City of El Reno, to take some pictures of the theater today. As we passed through the glass doors that lead into the theater, it was like taking a step back in time. The Art Deco style was carried out inside the building as well as on the exterior. The old concession stand is still in place as if it's ready to serve moviegoers. We were shown into the theater area. With all the lights on, the theater still appeared dim, which only helped to cast an eerie feeling around the room. After I made my way down to the front of the theater, I ascended the stairs to stand on the stage. When you stand on the stage, you can really get a sense of how large the theater truly is. Today, the Centre only seats 250 to 300 people, less than half the number it originally seated. I can only imagine how massive the crowds must have been during the Centre's glory days.

My first visit to the theater was several years before when I was looking for some local sites to set up one of our paranormal events. I had heard that the theater was haunted, and I was curious to learn more about it. I spoke to one of the members of the local theater group that was currently running stage productions out of that location and asked him if he had heard or experienced any paranormal activity. He told me about a time he had been alone upstairs in the office area and heard a noise coming from the lobby

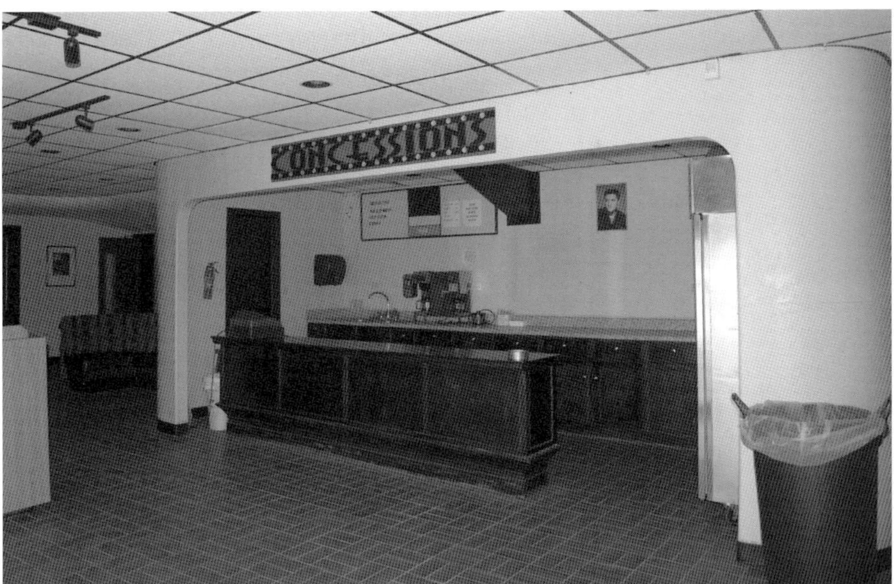

Concession counter at the Centre Theatre. *Courtesy of Tanya McCoy.*

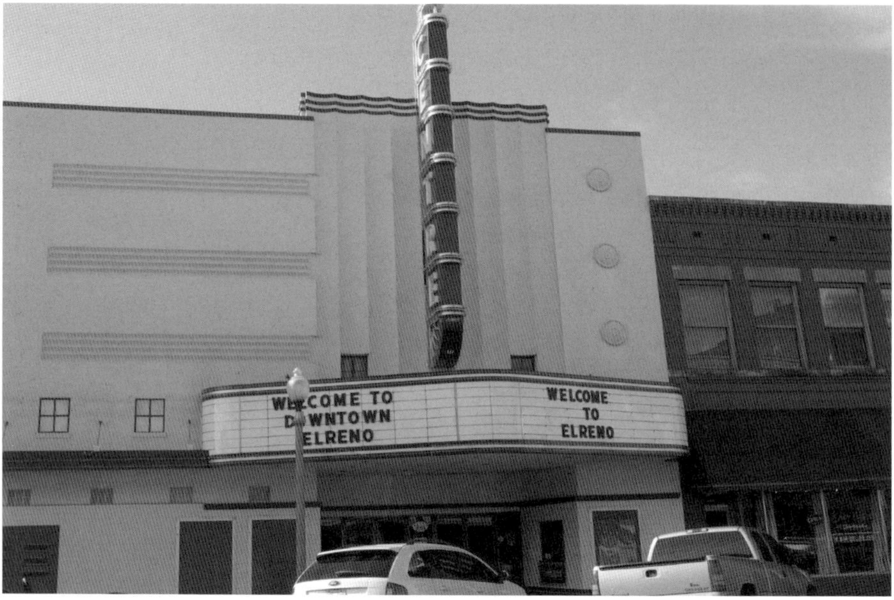

The Centre Theatre. *Courtesy of Tanya McCoy.*

area. He went downstairs to see who had come into the building, but no one was there. People often report seeing a man up in the projector room. The day of my first visit, I took pictures around the sitting area. When I reviewed them, It was surprised to see what appeared to be a man sitting up in one of the blue theater seats looking down at us. There was not a man with us that day other than the theater representative, and he was standing directly next to us. Prior to taking the picture, we had heard some noises coming from up in that area, but we didn't think much about it until we noticed the man in the picture. Some people believe it may be the spirit of Red Slocum, the man who reopened the theater in 1945 after a fire damaged the location and who spent many years of his life at the theater.

The theater spent several years empty until the city took over the building. Renovations were done, and once again the Centre Theatre was open for public use. For a short time, the El Reno Community Theatre group held various stage productions in the building until it moved into the El Reno High School auditorium to do its productions. The city now rents out the location for events and hosts a classic movie night open to the public. Once again, anyone wishing to enjoy a classic on the big screen, while enjoying a tub of movie theater popcorn, can kick back, relax and watch the films of yesteryear. Various other events are also held on site, should you find yourself looking for something to do on a weekend night. While you're there, make sure to keep your eyes and ears open; you never know who or what you might encounter.

DEAD MAN'S CURVE

It seems like every town has a legend of a crybaby bridge or a dead man's curve; El Reno is no different. What I find so interesting is that when you do an Internet search on haunted locations in El Reno, not many stories come up. El Reno actually has several haunted locations, enough that we plan on writing our next book on the city of El Reno. You won't find many stories talking about the Centre Theatre or even the Canadian County Historical Museum on many websites. However, the story that I did come across several times was about dead man's curve. The small, two-lane back road is located just behind the old sewage plant, built in 1941, that now sits abandoned, with the buildings overrun by Mother Nature. A heap of metal sitting in decay, buildings with broken windows and bricks and mortar lie fallen on the ground. This location possesses not only an eerie beauty but also a danger to anyone who might think about trespassing on this site.

There have been several different versions of what might have occurred at the location. One such version is that a van with nineteen people in it was traveling down the road when the driver tried to take the curve too fast. He lost control of the van, causing a wreck that killed all nineteen passengers. Another version of the story is that the van only had nine passengers in it when it wrecked. Such is the nature of most urban legends.

It is said that if you park along that road on a quiet night, you can hear the screeching of tires and the grinding of metal, as if a vehicle is being torn apart. Some say you can still hear the screaming of the victims as they lay dying along the roadside. Is the memory of the incident etched into the road? Perhaps the replay is a caution to those who still travel the dangerous curve.

Whether it is purely a legend or truth, the fact remains that the road is very dangerous and has seen many accidents throughout the years. Should you attempt to seek out the truth behind the legend to see if you too can hear the bloodcurdling screams of its victims, take caution. Your speed may not be the only thing you need to watch out for on Dead Man's Curve.

THE HUNCHBACK OF ROUTE 66

There is a second legend that surrounds another road in El Reno, one that passes by the town—a well-known highway once used as a main road across the United States. Route 66 was established on November 11, 1926, and stretched for 2,448 miles from Chicago, Illinois, to Santa Monica, California. The highway was one of the mainstreams used during the 1930s dust bowl era, when families tried to find their way west to California in search of making a better living. It later became a very popular vacation route for those who wished to experience a scenic drive across America, and it still is today. Also known as the "Mother Road," this popular highway inspired the legendary song "Get Your Kicks on Route 66," first produced by Capital Records in 1946 and performed by several artists such as Nat King Cole and Chuck Berry. This stretch of highway also inspired a hit TV show called *Route 66*, about two American drifters traveling along the famous route. The show first aired in 1960 and lasted for four years, receiving a few Emmy nominations. The most noted Emmy nomination was to a guest star on the show, Ethel Waters. It was the first Emmy nomination for an African American actress.

On a long stretch of the historic highway between El Reno and Weatherford comes the legend of the hunchback man. Many people have claimed to see the man. Some have even claimed to have given him a ride, but no one seems to know where he came from or why he chose to walk this long, lonely highway. He is seen wandering the road on rainy or cloudy nights. He wears a long brown trench coat with a Bogie-style hat pulled down over his eyes to help shield the rain from his face, or so the story goes. One unlucky driver ran into him one night—literally. The woman and her son were driving down the highway when she saw the man directly in front of her car. She tried to swerve but was too late. They both felt the impact of the car hitting him and immediately pulled over to check on the victim, only to find no trace of him and no damage to the car.

Another driver reports driving along the road when he came upon a man walking along the roadside in the rain with his brown coat pulled tightly around him. He stopped and offered the man a ride. He states he drove with the man for a while, sharing his love of God and witnessing to him. Suddenly, the man was gone without a trace. Yet another driver claims he also picked up the wandering stranger along the road on a wet, rainy night. He says his passenger was an eerie old man who never spoke a word to him. The peculiar passenger suddenly grabbed for the door handle in an attempt to jump out. The driver quickly pulled over, but the man had disappeared from his seat. The driver passed him once again a few miles down the road.

Did the man in the trench coat originally pass away after being hit by a car so many years ago? Does he continue to relive that same tragic night? Should you ever find yourself driving down this stretch of the historic Route 66 on a cold, rainy night, you might want to keep your eyes open. You never know who you might run into on the road. Perhaps you, too, will see the famous hunchback of Route 66.

YUKON

The Stage Door Theatre

Tucked away in an old residential area in Yukon, Oklahoma, sits an old historic building. Laughter used to fill the walls of the building when it once housed the Stage Door Theatre. For thirty years, the cast members and crew brought thousands of people to laughter and tears until the theater's most recent closing in 2016. I was blessed to be part of the last play produced in the old building, and I have personally had several experiences over the years both behind stage and throughout the building.

This historic building was built in 1907 as one of Yukon's original schools. In the mid-1980s, the Stage Door Theatre formed and began its lease of the old building. This two-story building, consisting of several large and small rooms as well as a large basement, has fallen into severe decay. The roof having several leaks has caused mold to grow throughout the building. Panels that once lined the ceilings now lie in crumbled piles throughout the building as the paint bubbles and peels from the walls. It was in this building that I first began my career in paranormal research.

When I first entered the building in 2008, I knew it had activity. You could feel the energy in the air. Up until then, I had only read about the paranormal. I had my first paranormal experience at the age of six years old, and since then, I had been curious about the paranormal field. Although I had always had an interest in the field, I had never had the opportunity to

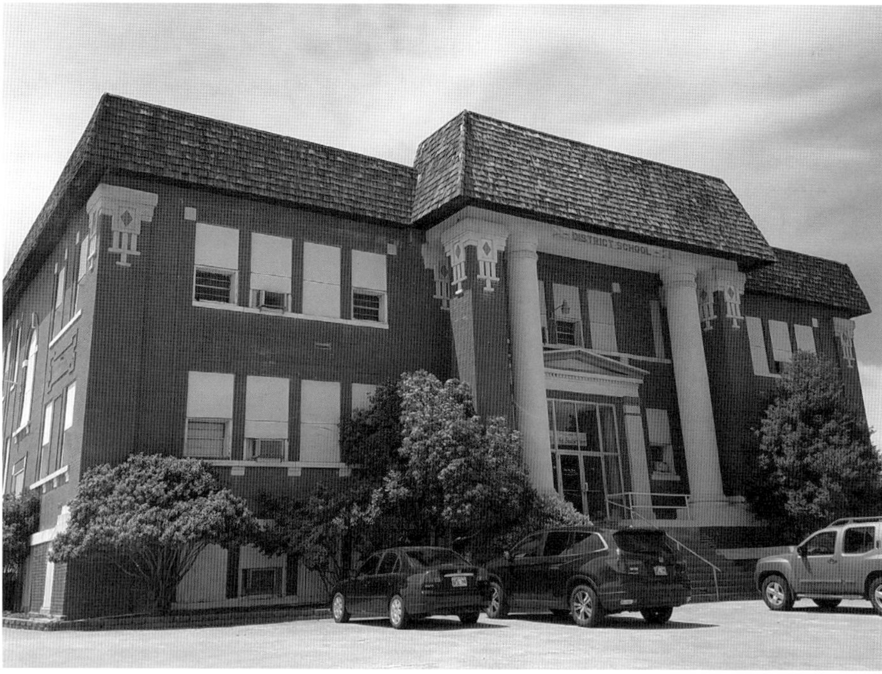

The Stage Door Theatre. *Courtesy of Tanya McCoy.*

participate in research. Little did I know that when I walked into that old brick building, my entire world was about to change.

I hadn't been involved with community theater since I was a teenager in California, and I decided it would be fun to get involved again. I took my teenage daughter to the local community theater to audition for a role for the upcoming play. I can still remember the feelings I got when I first stepped into the old building. There was no mistaking the fact that this building was haunted. I still remember the look on Rosemary's face as she led me and my daughter up the stairs. I asked her point blank if the building was haunted. She simply turned to me and smiled. To me, that was answer enough.

After my daughter was cast in the play, I, too, became part of the theater. I joined the board of directors and soon made several new and wonderful friends. It was there that I joined my first paranormal team. A group of the theater people started a group of like-minded individuals who were all interested in the paranormal. The new local group was known as DUST (Discovering and Understanding Supernatural Theories). Jamie McGuckin, one of the group's founders, approached me and asked if I would be interested in joining the team. I gladly accepted. Throughout the two years I was associated with the team, we often investigated the old building. Through those years, we had several experiences.

The current building was not the first one built on the site. Another school was built on the same property prior to 1907, but it burned down. We are unsure if anyone passed away on the current property, but we do know that several spirits inhabit the building. There have been several reports of disembodied voices, full-body apparitions and knocks heard throughout the building. Among these spirits is a little boy that we called Bobby.

Bobby has often been seen running around the basement area, which used to be the school's gym area, but he didn't stay only in that area. When I was teaching medical assistance students, some asked to go along on an investigation. I decided to take a group along one night to show them how we ran our investigations. That night, Bobby was feeling very friendly. A group of us was sitting down in the basement. One of my students named Tia was looking down the hallway toward the large back rooms when she and I saw Bobby run across the hall. He was a small slender boy dressed in early century clothing that reminded me of a newspaper boy. He had dark black hair and was around six to eight years old. It was the first time I had ever seen Bobby. She and I turned to each other in pure shock as we both confirmed what we had just seen. Years later, I was going through some old photo SD cards when I found something I had missed all those years ago. In a photo taken in an upstairs room, staring back at me was the small pale white face of Bobby.

Bobby was not the only spirit that resided in the building. Other cast members have reported being alone in the building working upstairs in the costume area when they heard someone knocking on the door. When they went to answer the door, no one was there. One director reported that when she was leaving the building one night, she had an eerie feeling and turned around to see a woman in period costume staring back at her from the glass door. Another spirit that was often felt and heard was one of a little girl. I had been alone in the building one day to set up for an event we were doing there. I had stepped into the restroom when I suddenly heard the giggle of a little girl coming from the other stall. The building was completely empty, and the doors had remained locked. There have been several spirits and occurrences noted around the building, but one of the most noticed ones was that of a dominant male figure. Many people reported feeling what seemed to be a strong presence, even authoritative, mainly onstage or in the green room area. At one point, I saw an older man in his mid-fifties standing onstage with his arms crossed over his chest simply staring out at me sitting in the audience area. I always felt like he was an authoritative figure like a teacher or principal, one who demanded respect.

The strangest occurrence happened the same day I heard the little girl giggling. While I was setting up for the event, I noticed an older woman standing outside staring up at the building. I went outside to see if I could offer any assistance. A younger woman got out of the car, and I introduced myself and asked if I could help with anything. "I brought my mom by to see her old school. I am helping her with her memoirs, and this was her old school," she told me. I asked them if they would like to come and tour the building, to which they both happily replied, "Yes!" I brought them in through the main doors and showed them around the old building from top to bottom. After the tour, I turned to the older woman and asked, "By the way, was the school haunted when you went here?" "Not that I know of," the lady replied. I told her about the authoritative man I had seen there before and have often felt in the building. I was a little surprised when the lady told me about a principal they had at the school who hanged himself. Was he the man I had seen on the stage that day?

The scariest encounter I have ever witnessed occurred during one of the last investigations we held there. We decided we would do a fundraiser for the theater and host a public ghost hunt just before the building was due to close. We had a large group with us that night, so we had broken up into several teams and split up into different areas throughout the building. At the end of night, my group was in the main theater area. Something decided it wanted to interact with us, but this was one spirit we had never encountered before. At first it tried to show itself as a young boy around the same age as Bobby. We soon learned that what we were dealing with was much more sinister.

I was sitting up on the stage along with a few other guests looking out into the audience section of the theater. A few other guests were scattered throughout the auditorium, sitting in various sections. To the back of the room were the exit doors, which led out into the central lobby of the building. The room was very dark, with only one small red light to help illuminate the area. One lady sitting in the front row became very upset. She said she could see the face of the child, but it had changed. It now had dark eyes and razor-sharp pointed teeth and was staring directly at her, and then it simply disappeared. She seemed genuinely upset and kind of shaken up by what she claimed to have seen. We often have people join us on events who claim to be sensitive, and a lot of us are, so I generally don't try to discredit them, but this report seemed a little far-fetched to me. Several of us onstage started to notice a dark shadow moving back and forth as if pacing in front of the doors. At that same instant, several people started complaining of headaches, myself included. Two ladies sitting next to each other out in the auditorium suddenly became very ill. I could see the shadow standing directly behind them. I grabbed my camera and took a picture in their direction. Later, when I pulled up the picture on my computer, I saw something dark standing in the middle of the picture. When I zoomed in on it, I was shocked to see the face that was staring back at me. It appeared to be a small boy about four feet tall, with dark eyes and razor-sharp pointed teeth. We've not been able to investigate the building since it closed its doors in June of that year. I'm still curious to know who or what that was that we all witnessed that night. Maybe one day we will be able to return to try to solve the mystery of the sharp-toothed creature.

So many spirits have come and gone through the old Stage Door Theatre. Not only did it house our theater group, but it also housed the Yukon Historical Society, which filled its rooms with personal items from residents who had passed as well as a military tombstone. The building also housed the Yukon Veterans Museum. This museum was made up of a collection of personal military memorabilia collected throughout the years. It housed various items, such as the medical bag and surgical instruments of Yukon's first medical doctor, as well as several pieces of equipment from his office. The theater group's stage props, clothes and costumes come from previous owners bought from around the area. How many of these items could have had energy attached to them? We may never know the exact number of spirits that resided or may even still reside at this historical location, but I personally hope that one day someone might restore this old building to its glory days and once again welcome laughter and life within its walls.

THE YUKON VETERANS MUSEUM

The Yukon Veterans Museum, now located at 1012 West Main Street in Yukon, Oklahoma, was once housed in the same building as the Stage Door Theatre. After the building closed its doors, the museum was forced to find a new location to help house and showcase its military memorabilia. It is now housed in a larger space with volunteers who spend hours upon hours gathering donations and artifacts and properly cataloging them. It is a

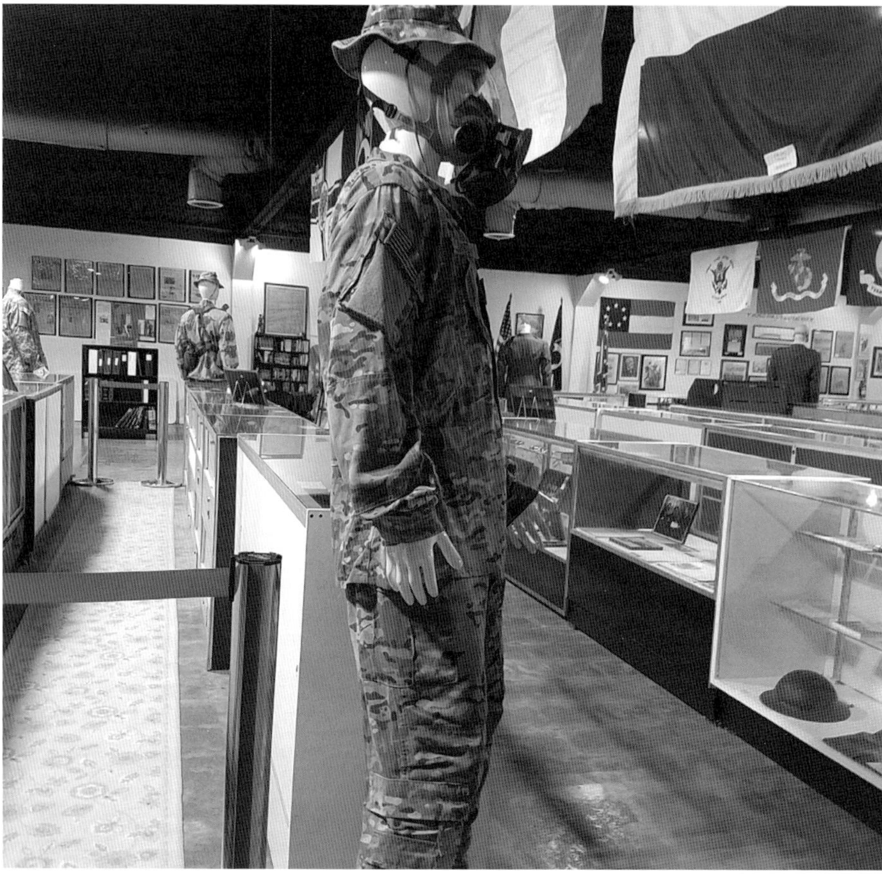

Yukon Veterans Museum. *Courtesy of Tanya McCoy.*

large open floor plan with rows of glass cases showcasing military weapons, foreign currency collected from previous wars and other personal items of our military heroes from all the previous wars. Once a month, volunteers come in to assist veterans filing paperwork for disability or offer advice on any other services they might need. The volunteers are men and women from all stages of life and nationalities who have banded together for one common cause: to defend our country and secure our freedom. I honestly can't tell you if this location is haunted or not, but I can tell you that if you are a history buff or just want to sneak a peek into the life of a true hero, stop by the museum and take a step back in history. While you're there, thank a vet for their service and their sacrifice to help provide the freedom you have today.

COTTONWOOD MANOR

Cottonwood Manor was originally built in the 1950s in Yukon, Oklahoma. Some people say it was a nursing home; others claim it was an insane asylum. In truth, it was a facility for patients who suffered from physical and mental disabilities. It was located in the middle of a residential area of the city, surrounded by single-family homes. The building stayed open until July 2001, when the state shut it down due to recurring and serious deficiencies jeopardizing the health and safety of the residents. The facility was built to house up to seventy-five clients but had up to two hundred at one time. When the doors were closed in 2001, there were eighty-eight residents who had to be placed in various other facilities. After years of neglect, the building started to fall apart. The halls still contained recliners and old toys scattered about. An old rusty swing set stood in the yard, with no one left to swing on it.

The building sat vacant for many years, tempting thrill seekers and vandals to have their way with it. It was a common place for teenagers to break into looking for something to do and hoping to find a little excitement. This, in turn, prompted several ghost stories and caused the building to be labeled as "haunted." I myself had never been to the location, especially since it goes against my team's rules and beliefs about trespassing on private property. Still, many have, and some came away with stories to tell about it.

I spoke to a young man named Blaine who claims to have had such an experience while exploring the old building. "It was pretty dark in there," he said as he started to share his story. "There was crap thrown everywhere; if you weren't careful, you'd trip on something." He told me how he and a few of his high school friends got bored one night and decided to check out the place. "I heard it was haunted," he said, "but I never did buy into that stuff much." With nothing much to do on that Friday night, they loaded up into one of their cars and headed out to the location. "We were there for about an hour, and nothing much had happened. We were just sitting around and talking about different stuff when one of my friends noticed something at the end of the hall. It was a bright light just kind of sitting there. We all started to freak out. We knew that cops have caught kids here before, and we knew we had been busted. Jimmy decided we should all make a run for it, so we jumped up and started running down the hall. We could see the light coming toward us, and we all started to panic. Two of us broke off from the group and headed down a separate hallway. We were hiding behind the door as we saw the light pass us. We were looking out through the crack of the door expecting to see a cop following the others, but there was no one there. It was just a ball of light floating through the air. Neither one us knew what to think. We just looked at each other, trying to figure out what we had just seen. We stepped out into the hall to take another look, but it was gone."

Later that night when the boys all met up again, Blaine tried to tell the other guys what he and his friend had witnessed. Despite having seen the light for themselves, they believed that Blaine was simply trying to play a trick on them. Blaine never returned to the site again.

Another report was made by someone who had never gone into the building but lived near it. She states that her family had purchased their first home in the same neighborhood as Cottonwood Manor. She claims she never felt quite "alone" in her own home, always feeling like she was being watched. She says that strange things would occur around her house—things she just couldn't explain. She never liked to be home alone and would avoid going to her house whenever possible. Her family soon sold the house and moved away. She claims she has had no further occurrences or feelings of uneasiness since they left that home. She also claims that people will move into the area but move out again after a short period. She says that you can always see houses for sale in that area no matter the time of year. She never wishes to return.

I spoke to another young lady about her experience at the location. She and her friends had visited the site in hopes of witnessing some paranormal activity of their own. They would not leave disappointed. She told me of her experience and how it would affect her for many years to come.

It was in late fall, only a few years after the building had closed. It was nearing Halloween, and she and a group of friends were looking for something fun to do. They had heard about an abandoned place in Yukon that was possibly haunted. Since they were living in Oklahoma City at the time, Yukon wasn't that far for them to drive, so they decided to try to locate the building. They parked their car a few blocks away and walked to the building. "We walked around the building, just checking things out. The place was a mess, with spray paint on the walls and dirt all over the place. We walked back to what looked like the old kitchen area and decided we would stay there to see if we could see anything. One of my friends brought a Ouija board with her, so we thought we would try it out." They set up the board in the old kitchen area and started their session. They started asking various questions, but not much seemed to be happening—at least they thought nothing was happening. When they started to leave, they heard a loud scream coming from behind them. "At first, we thought it was just someone trying to play a prank on us, but when we called out, no one answered. We decided to leave, so we packed up and started heading down the hall. We heard what sounded like footsteps coming from behind us. We turned around, but no one was there. We started running out of there as quickly as we could. When we reached the end of the hall, we heard what sounded like crying coming from down the hall. We left and never went back."

Since our team has never investigated the site, I can't give you my personal opinion on whether the building was truly haunted. I can tell you there were several state reports about neglect at the facility. One such report was about a woman who passed away from exposure. The seventy-four-year-old resident had wheeled herself outside and fallen out of her wheelchair. The facility claimed she could have only been outside for fifteen minutes, but the medical examiner stated in his report that due to her body temperature, she had to have been left outside for at least two hours. Another story associated with this location was about a special needs adult who passed away. He had spent a lot of his life there but did not pass away at the location; he had been moved to another facility prior to his death. The reason is unknown, but the facts about his death are truly heartbreaking. An article was written about his death and told the sad story of how someone can easily slip through the cracks when there is no one there to speak for him.

In 1993, a resident by the name of Jones passed away. Jones was a sixty-three-year-old mentally handicapped resident who had no family or friends to speak of. Those who knew him said he was a sweet guy, but he had a speech impediment, so communication was difficult for him. He had spent all of his life in institutions, never having a real home to speak of. Despite everything, people said he was always cheery and appreciative. The day he passed away, no one came to claim the body. His remains were sent to a local funeral home in Oklahoma City, where his body lay in limbo for months. With no friends or family to make arrangements for him, there were no funds to bury him. Months later, a state employee learned of how Jones's body still remained at the funeral home. The director of the funeral home tried everything he could to locate a relative but was never able to find anyone. The state employee pushed until she obtained funding to cover Jones's funeral costs. After seventy-five long days, his body was finally put to rest.

What really happened at this location? Did abuse occur like it does at so many other nursing homes, or was it another case of understaffed, underpaid employees due to steep budget cuts? Being a nurse for the past twenty years, I have seen and heard a lot, not just about patient abuse but about caregivers who truly love and care about their residents. With the good always comes the bad, and with death or abuse often comes some type of haunting, whether it be an intelligent haunting or just a photographic haunting. Do I believe this location could have been haunted? Yes, I do. Every nursing home I have ever worked in has been. For those of you who might want to check this place out, I can tell you, it is too late for that. A few years back, the city bulldozed the building due to the increase in trespassing and vandalism. Now, all that exists are the stories of what used to be and what no longer is.

Foreman Road

Foreman Road is a two-lane, unstriped back road that stretches from Eleventh Street in Yukon to Route 66 where it merges west of town in El Reno. During my high school years, Foreman was considered the "back way" to get into Oklahoma City. I think this was the preferred way for my parents to send me to the city without sending me on a highway. By day, you will find the road lined by some old farmhouses, a really great old grain silo and wide expanses of farmland. I preferred to take this road during the day. By night, it has a definite creep factor. For one, streetlights are scarce or nonexistent once you pass the short grouping of homes and elementary school just east of Shepherd heading toward Yukon.

On three occasions as I was making a night trip to Oklahoma City, there were strange occurrences. The first time, I was driving my 1985 Ford Mustang GL. It was a quiet night at the end of winter, so it was still cold outside. The trees lining the side of the road looked like skeletons with no leaves, and the cloud cover limited the moonlight that usually shone through onto the open fields. As I came to a narrow bridge over a small creek and surrounded by a wooded area, my radio started to skip around with intermittent static. Annoyed, I turned it off, and a few short seconds later, I lost all lights. Dash lights, radio and headlights all turned off. A little startled that something was wrong with my car, I slowed to pull over. As I was slowing, as quickly as they had gone off, all lights came back on, and there were no more issues for that drive. I mentioned the incident to my parents, and they checked the obvious—fuses, battery (which was new) and alternator all were in working order.

The second occasion was during the middle of summer. I had wrecked my Mustang, so I was driving a Chevrolet Cavalier Z24 convertible. I had made the trek from El Reno to Yukon down Foreman Road several times after the first incident with no issue, so I thought nothing of it, aside from the normal eerie feeling I always had on this road at night. This time, I was not listening to the radio and the moon was full and bright, reflecting off the crops in the fields on either side of me. As I reached the bridge, a feeling of being watched swept over me, and at the same time, I lost all lights again. This time I thought, OK, this is weird. Again, just as before, as I slowed to stop, the lights came back on. Although this time I was a little shaken up, there was no further incident.

The third instance occurred just before I moved from El Reno. This time, I was driving a newer Nissan Altima on my way to work in Yukon. For the third time, at the same location, I lost all lights in the car, only for them to turn back on and function fine the rest of the trip. I moved from

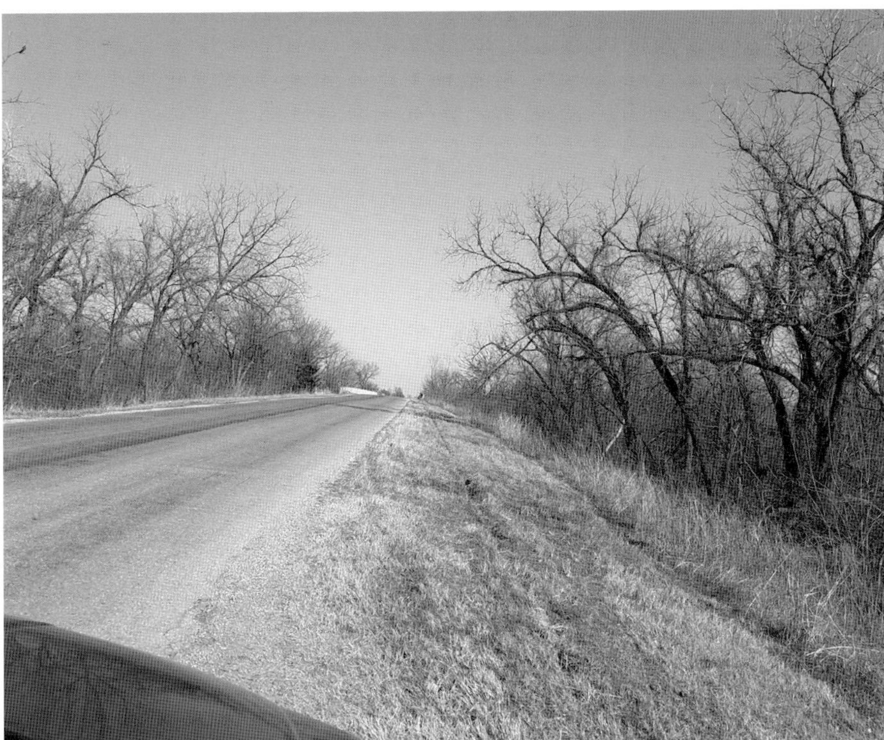

Foreman Road. *Courtesy of Tanya McCoy and Whitney Wilson.*

El Reno in 2006, so driving on Foreman Road after that was few and far between. I mostly pushed my experiences to the back of my mind; after all, I'd never heard anyone else talk about similar ones, just the eerie vibes of the road at night.

It wasn't until I started researching for this book that I spoke with a friend, Cara Pershall, an Oklahoma native, and found someone who had shared a similar experience. Cara had also lived in El Reno for a time. She spoke of two teens who lost their lives in a car accident around the S curve just a little west of my experiences. She has heard travelers on the road report seeing apparitions of the wandering teens and has seen them herself. The electrical disruptions and radio interference, however, are reported just east of the S curve near the narrow bridge, and Cara has also experienced these on numerous occasions.

It's been a while since I have driven down Foreman Road at night. During the day, it looks much like it did twelve years ago when I used it regularly. Is there a ghostly presence causing the car disruptions? Could it be explained by some natural source in the area? I'm not sure we'll get an answer to those questions, but I can say that nowadays, I take the highway.

MUSTANG

The Mustang Historical Society

Mustang, Oklahoma, became a small community after the land run of 1889. The first post office was established in 1895 and was named Mustang, giving the town its name. Mustang was once known for its bountiful crops. Agriculture was the mainstay for many years, but now there is little farming left in the area. Mustang has gradually becoming a suburb of Oklahoma City, with more families moving in weekly. Very few historical landmarks exist today in Mustang. The dirt streets and wooden sidewalks gave way to new land developments, and soon the face of Mustang would be changed forever. From the horse and buggy days to a five-lane highway, Mustang has seen a multitude of changes throughout the years. What history still exists is now housed in the Mustang Historical Society Museum.

Located in the heart of Mustang at 470 West State Highway 152 sits the old police station, municipal department and fire department. Built in 1969, the original structure only lasted a year. On May 7, 1970, a tornado hit Mustang, tearing the roof from the building and demolishing the adjacent shopping center. Carole Hanna, the local Mustang historian, states that Officer Lynn Steadman and a local drunk were inside the building at the time. The drunk slept right through the tornado while Officer Steadman held onto the cell door bars for dear life. The building was rebuilt soon after.

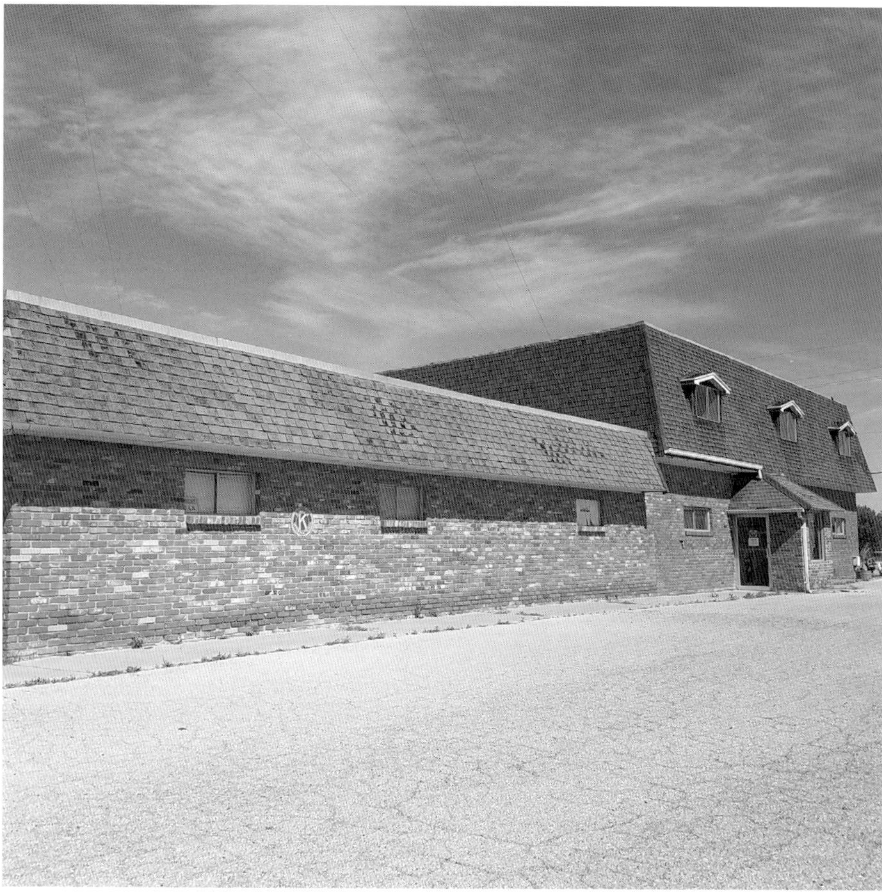

Mustang Historical Society Museum. *Courtesy of Tanya McCoy.*

The old square building with two large doors on the front where the fire engines used to be stored now houses something just as precious: history. Old wood paneling still lines the walls of rooms, and well-worn carpet is found throughout. Upstairs used to house various offices, as well as the courtroom. At one time, it even held a community closet to provide clothing for those in need. Many of the rooms upstairs are no longer in use due to a damaged roof that caused water damage in some of the rooms. Only one room remains in use today.

Downstairs, all the rooms are filled with collectables from current and previous residents of Mustang. Class photos line the walls dating from the early 1900s to more recent days. Those that can't be found hanging on the walls can be found in one of the many Mustang yearbooks. Various pieces of small farm and kitchen equipment are on display, and for those of you who like creepy dolls, there are even a few of those lying around. In fact, there is a small room dedicated just to them. Don't worry, there are some clowns as well.

One of the interesting pieces housed in the museum is an old pulpit from one of the local churches. When a large tornado hit the town of Mustang in 1927, the church was destroyed, but the pulpit was found several yards away in perfect condition. Several other rooms house various objects: an old travel organ, two old pianos and, my favorite, a bunch of old typewriters. The old 911 relay station is still housed in the building along with the two jail cells, complete with the old metal slabs as bunks with the plastic mattresses on top. Hanging between the two is an old-fashioned black-and-white striped prison suit, taking us back to the George Clooney movie *O Brother, Where Art Thou?*

The second set of rooms houses various objects from Mustang schools, an old cash register and one room depicting what a single-room house would have looked like back in the earlier days, complete with a queen-size metal frame bed, a hutch, a stove, table and chairs and a dresser; there was not much living space left to be had. Smaller rooms around the building house military memorabilia, Chisholm Trail history and Czech history from the local community. Toward the back of the building is a larger meeting room where various community groups meet, as well as the museum board. One such group is the local Kiwanis club, which hosts a food pantry and a toy drive during Christmas each year for the local community.

I personally believe most museums are haunted. How can they not be? They are filled with personal items, some very precious to the previous owners, which must contain some type of energy. The location of the museum is also a factor in the haunting. Just outside the Mustang museum sits a large antenna, which only helps to boost the EMF levels. To its southwest and southeast sit two cemeteries, and just across the street is the local funeral home. With that much energy and emotions being in such proximity, it would naturally make for a hot spot for paranormal activity.

We often investigate the Mustang Historical Society Museum, and over the years of investigating there, we have come across many different spirits. Each investigation brings a new experience to the ever-changing world of the paranormal. The most common spirit we run into at the Mustang Historical Society Museum is the woman we call Ms. Kitty. Ms. Kitty often resides in the one-room house, and she's not always in the most pleasant of moods. She doesn't take kindly to strangers messing with her stuff and often has no problem letting us know about it. She is often seen moving back and forth in the doorway of the room, shadowing out the light. She has responded using the lights of the Parascope and has even been seen using the FLIR. Her husband will visit from time to time, but he tends to be more mild tempered and is often just seen lying on the bed. The area is also known to have orbs (balls of light) seen several times with the naked eye. These weren't simple dust orbs caught on camera but full balls of lights seen flying around the room. High EMF levels are often noticed in the hallway just outside the room. The strangest EMF reading I ever obtained was off a book of S&H Green Stamps (Green Stamps were often given out by grocery stores after you purchased food and could be used like money to purchase various items). There shouldn't have been any energy levels coming off a stack of papers, but then someone had to lick the stamp to make it stick in the book. Was this perhaps why we were picking up on energy levels? Another item that tends to give off high energy levels is an old cash register that sits in the room just adjacent to Ms. Kitty's. When most of us think of cash registers, we think of the type used today: the electronic one. This cash register has no source of energy going to it. Perhaps it's the lights in the room giving off the reading. Several of us thought the same until we noticed that there was no reading coming from above or below the register; we only had hits on the keys, even when the lights were out. There are a few other items in the rooms that have had energy readings as well: an old 1800s doll, a piece of old jewelry and a brush, all located inside a glass case, also with no electricity present.

Upstairs, we often encounter several spirits: a lady whom we believe may be Native American, a little boy and one we call the angry man. The woman often comes in very sad. She's only showed up a few times for us, but when she does, it's usually with the same sadness and seems to reference abuse. The little boy is another character altogether. He is often seen playing in one of the rooms, but he will also travel to others. He appears to be around six years old and is very curious. His favorite piece of equipment to communicate with us is the touch lights. When we place the lights in the room he plays in, he will often answer us by turning on the light. The lights we use must be touched to come on. Simply walking by them will not set them off. He also will use our flashlights to answer by turning them off and on again. Several people have witnessed him during investigations, and he has even showed himself as a full-body apparition from time to time. He is playful, and no one ever feels threatened by his presence. That can't be said about all the spirits that reside here.

Another well-known spirit is known as the angry man. He doesn't like it when people come into his space, and he tends to let us know it. You can usually feel when he comes around. He is usually more aggressive to the men, and some have reported feeling him giving them a slight push. His presence is felt more in one of the back offices upstairs, one we don't investigate much due to water damage from the roof. When I first started investigating at the museum, I obtained a picture that showed the face of a man very plainly in one of the inside windows. He had dark brown hair and was balding on top. He wore glasses that would date back to the 1980s and was clearly in uniform. A badge was noticed on his chest. Could this be the man we have all been experiencing upstairs? One day I hope to be able to access the pictures of the police of Mustang's past to see if I can locate this unknown officer's name to finally put an identity to the spirit that we have been studying for so long.

Not all spirits that we run across at the museum stay there. With different objects being brought in from time to time, we often experience different hauntings. We had a larger group in one time while we were doing our events, large enough that we had to split into four different groups. My paranormal team often hosts events where we take people out to a known haunted location and teach them how to run a proper investigation in a safe environment. This night was one of those nights. A team leader led each group throughout the building, and we set up in various sites. This particular night, it was the old jail cells that seemed to be the most active for us. After each group toured, I would ask the members if they had witnessed anything and, if so, what it was. In the first group, one of the women felt like she was being strangled and she couldn't breathe. In the second group, another woman reported seeing a large black shadow hovering up in the corner of the wall of the jail cell. When the third group came through, the woman who reported witnessing something seemed visibly upset. She told me that she could see the legs of a man dangling at the top of the jail cell. None of the women had been in the same group or even heard each other's stories, but as their stories unfolded, what they had described could only be pieced together as the image of a hanging man. I asked Carole if she knew of any suicides or deaths in the jail, but she did not. She did tell me, however, that a few years earlier, a young man had hanged himself in a park not far from the building. Could this be his spirit lingering on? If so, why did he show up here, clearly where he didn't die? Or has there perhaps been a suicide or even murder that we are unaware of that might have taken place? Could this spirit simply be attached to an object located somewhere in the building, and did he just happen to show himself in the jail cell to not just one person but three?

The last room I would ever expect to get paranormal evidence in would be the meeting room. We often use that as our command center where we brief our guests, unload equipment and take breaks between rounds. One guest who joined us sent me an audio clipping that she obtained on her digital device while we were setting up one night. You can clearly hear us all talking about various things, and then I go into the introduction part of the night, where I go over the rules and regulations of our investigations. While I'm talking, you can clearly hear a small female voice say, "ghost," as if she walked up to the recorder and spoke directly into it in a joking voice. There were no small children present that evening, and no one acknowledged the statement or appeared to hear it.

My group was the first paranormal team to ever investigate the museum. I always felt drawn to the old building, and after being introduced to Carole, we were allowed in to investigate. No one had ever witnessed any paranormal activity, or if they had, they didn't realize what it was. After our investigations, I took several pieces of evidence we had caught up to the board to present them with what we had found. Carole has joined us on many investigations there, and she tends to be Ms. Kitty's favorite; she responded one night on the Ghost Radio saying that she liked it when Carole played music for her on the piano. Carole now greets Ms. Kitty when she walks in and often will play some gospel tunes for her. Many were still skeptical. While Carole was a little more open to the thought, Glenn, the president at the time, was not—at least until one day when he himself witnessed his own unexplainable event. He was in the building alone one

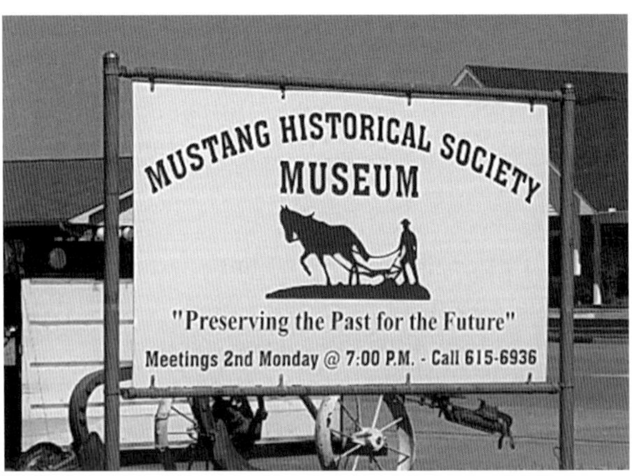

Mustang Historical Society Museum welcome sign. *Courtesy of Tanya McCoy.*

Saturday locking up after-hours. He had just locked the door when he felt someone grab him by the shoulder. He turned around, but no one was there. I think we may slowly be making a believer out of him.

We always enjoy investigating the Mustang Historical Society Museum. If you are ever in Mustang, stop in and say hello to Ms. Kitty and the gang. Just make sure you don't mess with her stuff!

Mustang City Hall

Mustang isn't as well known as Guthrie as a haunted city in Oklahoma, but it does have a few haunted locations, one of which may come as a shock to most. In July 2001, a storm came through Mustang, destroying city hall, and left the city in need of a new location. Officials soon chose a building to rent. They chose a building just off Highway 152, and the temporary city hall was opened. It wasn't a very large building; it was split into two large open rooms, with one side acting as the courthouse and the other as the city works offices. I can remember the feeling I used to get when I would walk in to pay my water bill. The space always seemed so dark and dreary. I had no idea at the time what the building had once been.

Not being born or raised in Mustang, I didn't know a lot of history about the town; I just knew that this building always seemed to intrigue me. I soon learned why. Prior to the city hall occupying the building, it had been a funeral home. I recently spoke with Gayla Early, an employee for the city, and she shared a few experiences she had while working in the building. Gayla said their part of the office was located in the old embalming room area. She spoke about the feelings she and others would experience in the building, such as the feeling of being watched and never quite being alone. There were reports of objects moving on their own, and shadow figures were even seen from time to time. In 2008, a new city hall was built, and the offices were moved.

Soon after, a new floral business took over the building. It wasn't long before the new owners and employees started experiencing paranormal activity of their own. After learning about the building's previous activity, I decided to contact the new owners in hopes of conducting an investigation. I spoke to the owner, and she began to tell me about some of the things they were experiencing. She told me about a lady who had come to visit the store and asked her about the little girl who was standing in the back corner.

She told the owner that she had psychic abilities, and she had seen this little girl standing there. No one knew who the little girl could have been or why she was haunting the location, but several people had reported seeing the same little girl. The location I was most drawn to had been to the west side of the store. This is where they would make their floral arrangements, as well as other goods. I felt what seemed to be a spirit of an older gentleman hanging out in the backroom area. I shared what I had felt and told them I saw him walking back into the room and then disappearing from sight. I was informed that the room I was referring to was the old embalming area. The owner agreed to let us come in to investigate, and a date was set. A few weeks had gone by, and I called to confirm the date for the investigation. The owner informed me that they couldn't go through with the investigation after all. She told me that since our last visit, activity had increased. Electrical issues started occurring, and for almost a week none of the cash registers would work. She felt the spirits were possibly upset by the thought of an investigation, and she wanted to keep them happy. The investigation never took place, and no further occurrences were reported from the store owner. In 2016 or 2017, the floral shop closed its doors.

The new city hall that was constructed in 2008 is a much larger building than before. When you enter the front door, you will see the city utility works office to the right and the court area off to the left. When I asked Gayla if they have experienced any activity since moving to the new building, I was quite surprised to hear that they had experienced one strange thing. A shadow figure was caught on one of the cameras in the courtroom while no one was in the building. Did one of the spirits from the old building choose to move on to the new one when the city did, or is this perhaps a different spirit altogether? The building may be newer, but the land has been around for a very long time. Maybe one day we will learn more about the ghost that haunts the city hall.

Riverside Cemetery

On the outskirts of Mustang, just to the side of an old country road, sits the small Riverside Cemetery. Not many people know of the cemetery, and those who do have lived in Mustang their entire lives. Many of the headstones date back to the beginning of the 1900s, prior to Oklahoma statehood. Some of our city founders are buried at this site, as well as some more modern-day

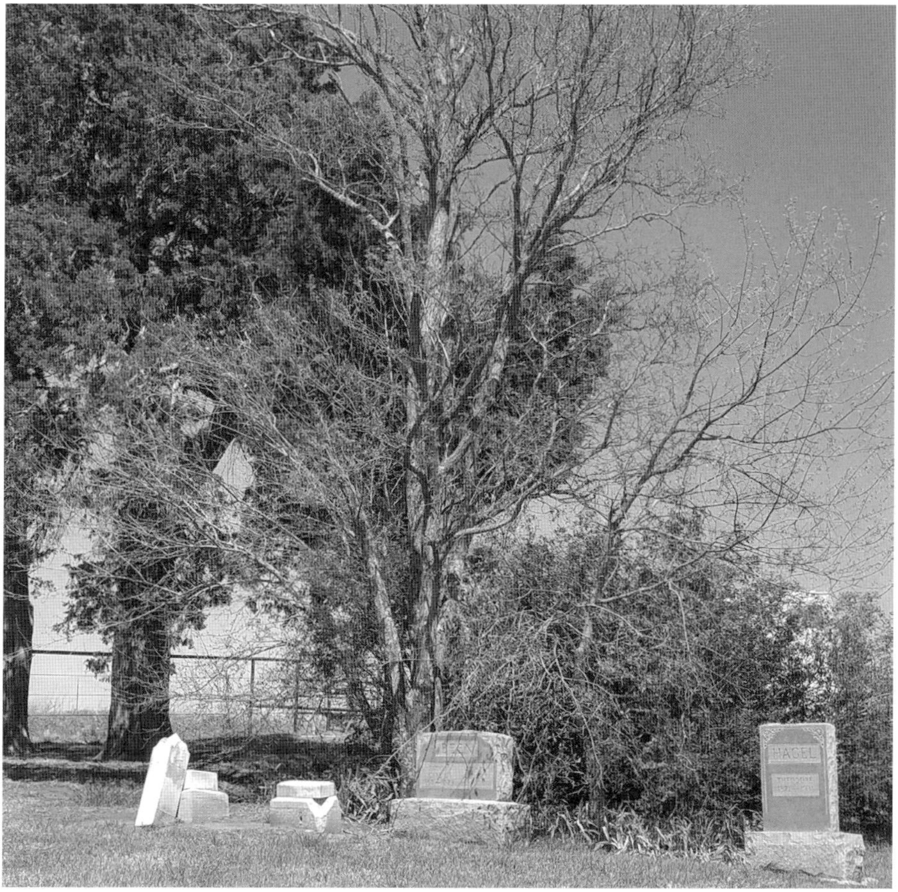

Riverside Cemetery. *Courtesy of Tanya McCoy.*

plots. It's a peaceful setting, surrounded by farmland that seems to stretch on forever. Even as the sun settles, sending its golden beams across the evening sky, this cemetery remains peaceful.

Despite the serenity of this cemetery, ghost stories still exist. One such story talks about a little girl who is seen running around the graveyard at night, as one eyewitness reports. She was driving to a friend's house late one night. She had never been there before and was trying to follow the directions her friend had given her. As she was driving down the road, she noticed a small girl wearing a flowery dress, skipping alongside the road. She thought it was strange since it was already getting dark. She figured the girl lived in one of the houses nearby and would surely head home soon. As she drove closer toward her, she started to feel as if something wasn't quite right about the situation. She pulled her car over and was about to ask the girl if she was lost or needed help. Then she noticed she could see right through her. It was then that she noticed the old headstones that lay just beyond the metal fence area. Slowly, the image of the little girl started to fade away. The driver put her car in gear and quickly sped away. She's not sure why she was so scared by the sight of the little girl. She claims she didn't feel threatened in any way; she was just caught completely off guard by the situation. She says she has driven down the road several times over the past few years but has never seen the little girl again.

Other reports of activity include unexplained lights floating around the cemetery at night and disembodied voices. When I was part of my original paranormal team, prior to forming OPA (the Oklahoma Paranormal Association), we visited the cemetery. We had heard various reports of the location being haunted, and we wanted to check it out for ourselves. It was a clear night; no clouds were present, but with it being Oklahoma, there was a slight wind. We ran audio recorders in hopes of catching a possible EVP and took several pictures around the cemetery. Despite feeling as if we were not alone, we did not witness any paranormal activity that night. Graveyards have always been popular sites for people to visit in hopes of witnessing some paranormal activity. Now that I look back at it, I wish I would have known what I know now—that despite a cemetery being open to the public, it is still private property. You should always get permission to enter a location prior to investigating, especially at night. It is still considered trespassing, and you can incur fines or even take the risk of serious injury.

Okarche

Holy Trinity Cemetery

Just over ten miles north of El Reno on Highway 81 sits a quaint Catholic cemetery, Holy Trinity. The cemetery is a small one, with a modest gate and tall juniper trees lining the perimeter. A really old cemetery—this one with graves from the 1800s—combined with the active imaginations of small-town teenagers is a recipe for an urban legend, such as the one of a witch named Sarah buried in Holy Trinity Cemetery.

The story goes that a witch named Sarah's final resting place was at this cemetery, and people who visited after dark would have paranormal experiences. As a curious group of teenagers, Jennifer Handley of El Reno and her friends decided to make the trip to the cemetery one Wednesday night. They pulled up to the cemetery, but the driver of the truck they were in would not get out. The others got out and entered the gate. It was said that the grave of Sarah glowed. As they walked toward the grave, one of Jennifer's friends was chanting, "Sarah…Sarah…Sarah…" About halfway to the grave, a blinding light illuminated the grave, so bright and startling that the group of friends turned tail and sprinted back to the truck. Terrified, they left the cemetery as quickly as possible. As they drove away, the sound of hands hitting the sides of the truck filled the cab.

After getting a decent distance away from the cemetery, in an attempt to be logical, they briefly discussed the events of the night. The light they

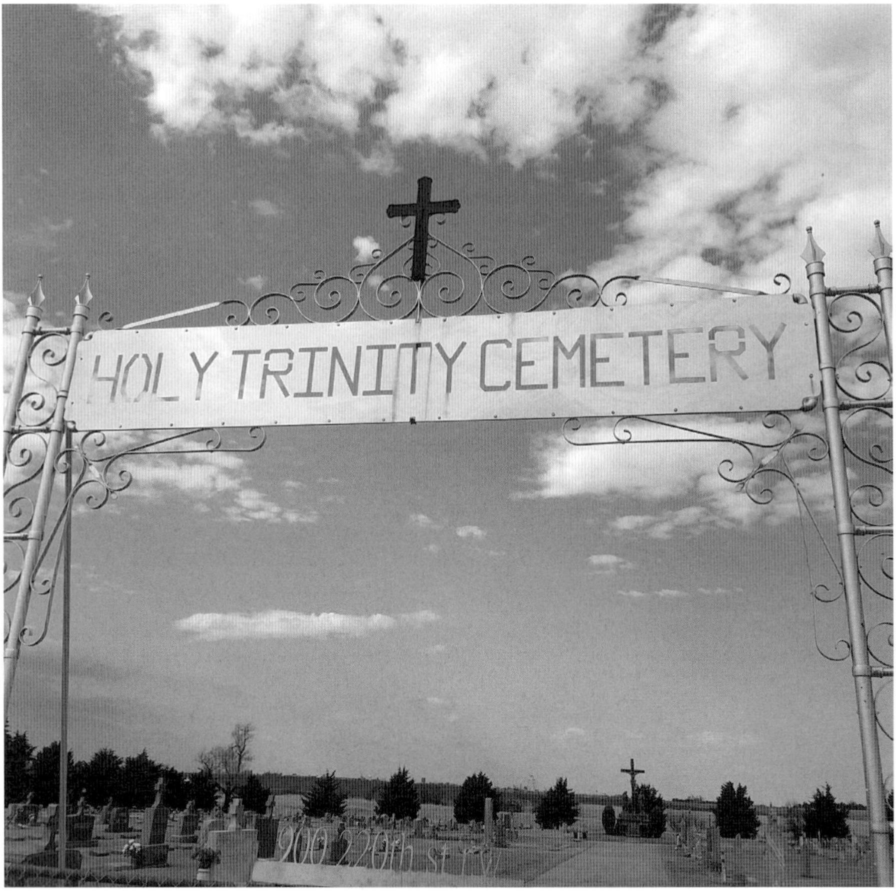

Holy Trinity Cemetery entrance. *Courtesy of Tanya McCoy.*

could not find an explanation for. One of the friends suggested that the banging could have been a speaker that came out of the bed of the truck, even though there were no marks in the paint or damage. They didn't return to that cemetery again.

I visited the cemetery during the day. The grounds are well kept. Some of the older headstones were missing parts of their etchings, which is to be expected with Oklahoma winds, weather and time. The wind whipping through the juniper trees around the perimeter surrounded the site in a sort of peace; after all, the trees themselves are symbols of cleansing and protection. The events of the past are not evident now, at least in the daylight. However, the memory is still very vivid for Jennifer, who looks back with a questioning

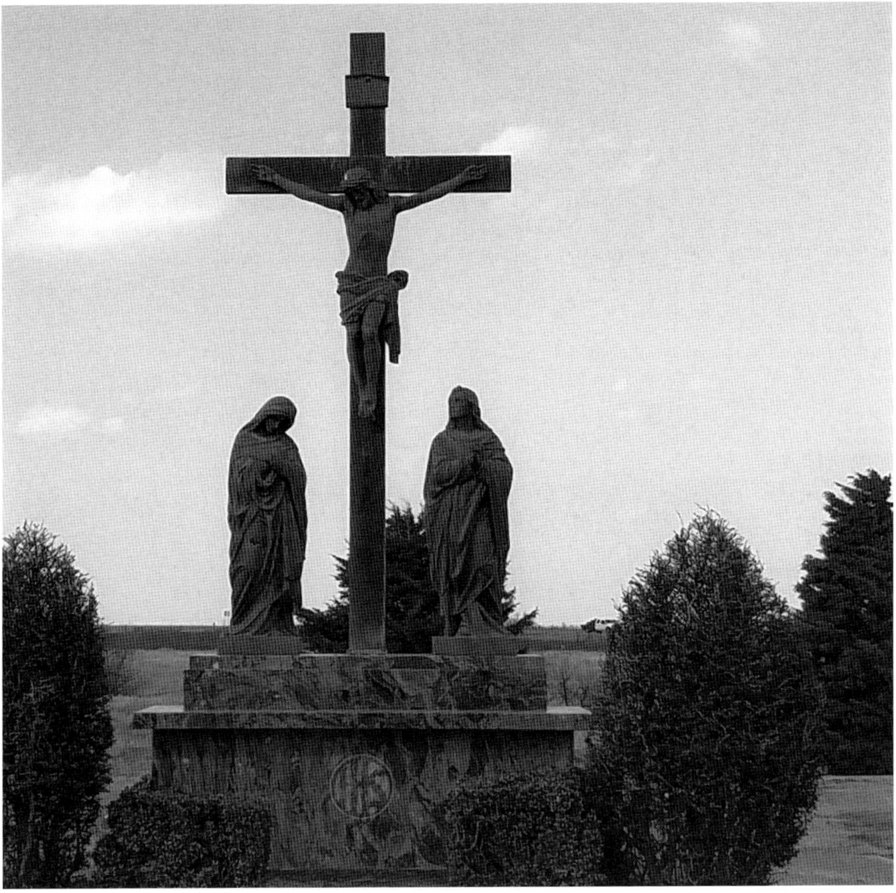

Holy Trinity Cemetery. *Courtesy of Tanya McCoy.*

mind. How do these legends begin? When do they end? Will we ever know who Sarah really was? Perhaps she was just misunderstood in life and simply reaching out from beyond the grave to those daring enough to approach an old cemetery at night.

I guess we have reached the point in this story where I tell you that cemeteries do, in fact, close at dusk, and trespassing is illegal. So please avoid the urge to seek proof of this legend without going through the proper channels.

Lake Overholser

Lake Overholser sits divided between Canadian County and Oklahoma County, with Canadian County to the west. Here you will find a floating dock that you can walk out on to fish, often catching small crappie or catfish, and perhaps once in a while you might get lucky enough to catch a small bass. A children's playground is just across the road, with ducks and geese running around the ponds and lake. This lake is a popular area for bike riders or motorists who just want to go out for a quick ride on a warm, sunny day. It is also a popular area for local joggers who enjoy a more scenic run.

Built in 1918, Lake Overholser was constructed to help provide an adequate supply of water for the water treatment plant. The city relied heavily on the North Canadian River as well as local ground wells for much of the city water. As population increased, so did the need for more fresh water. The idea for a man-made lake came into play, and construction began. In 1923, the Canadian County river flooded and inundated much of the city. It became very evident that a new dam, bigger and more efficient, was needed. Designed by Neils Ambursen and constructed by Ambursen Construction Company of New York, the dam sits 68 feet in height and 1,650 feet in length. It consists of buttressed spillways, a solid spillway, a concrete walkway across the dam and a brick-walled pump house.

The lake was named after Edward Overholser, sixteenth mayor of Oklahoma City and son of Henry Overholser, one of the founding fathers of Oklahoma City. Ed Overholser, born in Kansas, arrived in Oklahoma

City in 1890 and took over the running of the Overholser Opera House. He helped to organize the towns of Stroud, Wellston, Luther and Jones. He became a member of the school board and later the chairman of the board of county commissions for Oklahoma County. Lake Overholser is relatively small in size, its maximum depth only reaching thirteen feet, with an average depth around six feet and a surface area of around 1,500 square acres, making its shore length around seven miles.

Despite its size, it is still a great place to go sit next to the water, drop a line or jog a mile. It is considered one of the most scenic areas along the famous Route 66, which runs right through it. The days can be peaceful sitting on the shoreline, feeling the cool breeze being carried across the water, while the local wildlife goes about its daily musings. A duck can often be seen gliding across the water, dipping its head beneath the waves in hope of catching its next meal, while just a few feet away the sound of a small fish jumping up out of the water can be heard. It's a nice place to visit and take the kids for a fun day in the sun, but come nightfall, you may wish to pack up and leave. The lake can take on a new life all its own.

Lake Overholser will be turning one hundred years old in 2019, and over the past one hundred years, the lake has seen many tragedies. From strange lights to the ghostly image of a woman walking along the shoreline, this lake has no shortage of ghostly apparitions.

One such story comes from a man going by the name of Bill (who wishes to keep his full name left out at this time). Bill told me how he used to fish late in the evening just off the fishing dock. He would often sit and watch the sun go down, enjoying the peacefulness that seemed to settle across the lake. He shared with me his frightening experience he had in April 2003. That day was like any other day—at least he thought it was. He had just gotten off work. It had been a very stressful day, and he thought he would swing by the lake to do a little evening fishing to help relax before heading home. He often carried his fishing things in the trunk of his car since it was one of his favorite pastimes. Not being married at the time, Bill didn't find himself in a rush to get home, so he grabbed a few snacks and headed out to his favorite spot on the lake. The sun was just setting past the horizon. He was kicked back in his chair with his line in the water, just taking in the sounds of the water hitting softly against the rocks of the shoreline. With it being so early in the season, there weren't many people out around the lake, so it was a rather quiet evening. He was getting ready to pack up and head home when he noticed someone standing just down the shoreline from him. She was a pretty girl, around mid-twenties with long dark hair. She was staring

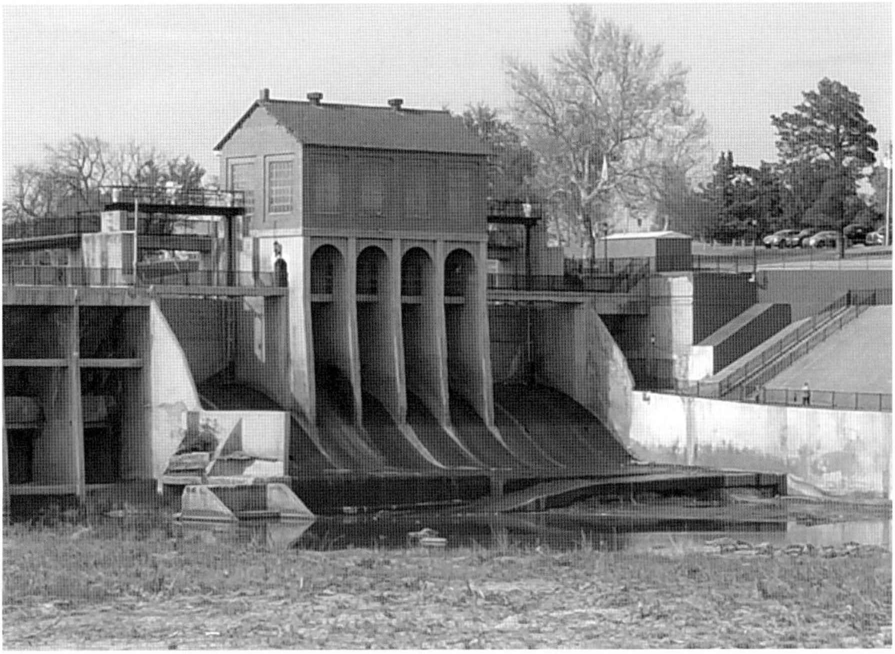

Lake Overholser Dam. *Courtesy of Tanya McCoy.*

off across the lake, as if she was deep in thought. "She seemed so sad," Bill told me. "With it getting so late and dark, I was worried about her being out there all alone." So he called out to her. He said he tried calling out several times, but she would never look over at him. He decided he would approach her to see if there was anything he could do or perhaps give her a lift somewhere since he didn't notice another car or person around her. He put his things into his car and then started to head over to her. He said he was about twenty feet away when he called out to her again. This time, she turned to look at him. He could see a thick line of blood running down the right side of her face. Their eyes met, and then she simply disappeared. There was no sound of a splash, no sound of running footsteps. Where had she gone? "I was scared to death," Bill told me. "I knew what I had seen, but I couldn't explain what had just happened. One minute she was there, and the next she was gone." Bill says he still goes out to the lake to fish, but he has never seen his ghostly lady since. But then again, when the sun starts to set, Bill packs up and leaves. No longer does he stay past nightfall, but he says to this day, he still wonders what or who he saw that night at the lake so many years ago.

The next encounter I learned about takes on an otherworldly type of paranormal experience. It comes from a young couple out to enjoy some alone time along the lake shore one night during the late hours of the evening. A young couple in their late teens decided to park out by the lake after catching a late-night movie and grabbing a bite to eat. They weren't ready to end their date just yet, so they thought a trip to the lake would be nice since it was a warm summer evening. They parked on the west side of the lake, looking out across the water. They had been there a little while and were enjoying looking out at the stars when they noticed a large bright light just above them. Thinking it was just another plane flying over, they didn't pay much attention to it. There was a small airport nearby, and seeing small planes overhead was not uncommon, especially on a clear night like this one. They continued on with their conversation, making plans to see each other the following weekend, when they happened to look up again. The same bright light was still there and had not moved positions. It was too large to be a star, and it was sitting too still to be a plane. All of a sudden, the light split off into three separate lights shooting off into three different directions in the night sky. They stayed at the lake for another hour or so to see if they could see it again, but the strange bright lights never returned.

These lights in the sky aren't the only strange lights ever reported from this lake. A few years back, a man was out riding his motorcycle around the lake, taking in the spring-like weather, quite early for the season. He was just rounding the turn by the dam when he looked out across the lake and noted a red ball hovering just above the water. He pulled over to the side of the road, trying to get a better look at what he was seeing out on the lake. There were not any boats on the water, and no one was fishing in that area. He could see the light's reflection on the water as it slowly came closer to him. He started to walk closer to the shoreline toward the light when he heard the screeching of tires and the sound of a truck engine close by. He turned to see a driver lose control of his truck, trying to take the curve too fast, and swerve to the side of the road right where he had been standing, missing his bike by mere inches. Had he not noticed the red light and walked over to get a better look, the truck would have hit him head-on. Was this mysterious light a warning or perhaps another spirit trying to help detour the biker from ending up injured or worse from the carelessness of another driver?

Since the lake opened, there have been many reported deaths at the site. From 2007 to 2013, reports ranging from accidental drownings to murder have been seen in local newspapers and on television. Are the spirits of the lake's victims still trapped here, or do they even realize that they have perished? Do they stay around to help warn others of possible impending death or perhaps protect them from meeting the same untimely death that they themselves have experienced? Do visitors from other planets frequent our skies, watching and observing us? Whatever reason there may be, a visit to Lake Overholser is a nice little getaway from the hustle and bustle of city life. Just make sure when you're there to keep your eyes open; you never know what or who you will see.

Cedar Lake

Just fifteen miles southwest of the town of El Reno sits Cedar Lake. It is a small lake with a small community. I spent many summer nights hanging out there with my friend who lived in a small house in the lake community. Much of the lake property is surrounded by large trees; in fact, I don't recall ever actually seeing the lake itself. I guess we were too busy mingling with other people to actually make it down to the lake. I did spend quite a bit of time meandering around the dirt roads. I remember one rainy night, it had been raining most of the day, and I barely made it up the steep driveway to my friend's house. The nights were quiet, aside from the occasional hoot from an owl or bustling from local wildlife. You could actually see the stars away from the light pollution in the city. It wasn't the lake itself that spawned the urban legend of a witch who practiced dark magic but the road leading to the lake.

The path to the lake has a few turns, including one that is nearly ninety degrees. I thought it was the fabled Dead Man's Curve, but no one knows for sure. At the time I was making the frequent trek to Cedar Lake, there were at least a couple of crosses placed at the side of the road near this area. It was after this ninety-degree left turn that things got interesting. The scenery changes from fields with roaming cows to large trees and rock embankments on either side of the road. Considering most of my trips were after dark, since I was a teenager and mostly worked the evening shift, it was quite creepy. I remember telling my friend the first time I visited her home that there was just something about that road that creeped me out.

She said that it had been rumored there was a witch who lived on that short stretch of road, set back away from the side of the road. The witch was said to have sacrificed children in her magic dealings. The house the witch lived in was burned to the ground and the witch hanged when it was found out what she had been doing. There was a small wooden shed-style building still standing but no other remnants of what was said to have gone on there. The gnarled trees growing on either side of the road reminded me of a movie, as if they were waiting for the right moment to come to life and swallow up any passersby.

The feeling on that road was heavy and like you were being watched. I looked straight ahead every time I drove it so as to not catch a glimpse of what might be lurking in the brush. Is it possible that my friend was just messing with me? Or perhaps whoever told her was messing with her? Who knows? What I do know is that I was not and still am not a fan of driving that stretch of road.

UNION CITY

Located just south of El Reno off Highway 81 and just west of Mustang off Highway 152 sits the quiet little town of Union City. In 1889, the post office was established, and one year later, Thomas and Mary Leslie filed for township. In 1890, the railroad arrived, causing a sudden boom in the population. Agriculture is the base for the economy in the small city. Union City has a population just under two thousand. The oldest building in town is the Richardson Building. This brick building was built in 1910 to be used as a bank. There was a report of one bank robbery in the town, during which no one was injured. A local resident was down on his luck and sought to rob the local bank as a means to an end. The building now sits vacant with boarded-up windows and door, falling victim to the elements. A small correctional facility is located just on the outskirts of the town, offering some economic stability to the town.

While I was unable to track down any firsthand paranormal accounts, there are several spots that have some interesting vibes. Union City and Sherman were known as twins. Sherman is listed as a ghost town in records at the Canadian County Historical Museum. However, according to the Union City town webpage, a section of town is still known as Sherman even after the merger. Union City offers a quiet community setting just minutes from Oklahoma City without all the hustle and bustle of city life.

Piedmont

Located in the northeastern part of Canadian County, just west of Oklahoma City, sits the small town of Piedmont. In 1903, Dr. E.H. Long initiated the townsite for Piedmont. An auction was held in 1904 for lot space in Piedmont for residential and business, which drew new people into the area. Another major attraction was the arrival of the St. Louis, El Reno and Western Railway, which helped connect Guthrie to El Reno. This brought in new residents and more business, and the area flourished. Then, in 1924, the railway pulled away from the Piedmont area, causing a decline in the local population. In 1950, the community hit an all-time low of 120 residents, making it seem like Piedmont was on its way to becoming another Oklahoma ghost town. The population started to rebound in the 1970s, with the expansion of Oklahoma City causing a major growth in the Piedmont area. Many Oklahoma City residents migrated to the Piedmont area in search of more affordable living.

Today, Piedmont is still a quiet community with a small-town feel but close enough to the metro area for easy access to work and shopping. We were unable to locate any haunted history or urban legends associated with the town. We did, however, come across an interesting bit of information while researching at the Canadian County Historical Museum. A somewhat eerie occurrence happened many years ago. One of the first doctors from Piedmont was traveling in south Oklahoma when his home caught on fire. Two hours later, he was killed in a car crash. We were unable to locate any further information as to the cause of the fire or car accident.

BIBLIOGRAPHY

Barker, Carolyn. "Burials in the Fort Reno Cemetery, 1874–1948." files.usgwarchives.net/ok/canadian/cemetery/ftreno.txt.

Canadian County Historical Museum Archives.

Canadian County Historical Society Museum. "Brinton Darlington and the Cheyenne-Arapaho Agency." canadiancountymuseum.com/brinton-darlington-and-the-cheyenne-arapaho-agency.

Dortch, Steven D. "Chisholm Trail." The Encyclopedia of Oklahoma History and Culture. www.okhistory.org.

Elks History Project. "How the Elks Began." www.elks.org/history/NewsStory.cfm?StoryID=71651.

Haunted Places in Oklahoma. "Dead Man's Curb." theshadowlands.net/places/oklahoma.htm.

———. "Route 66 to Weatherford." theshadowlands.net/places/oklahoma.htm.

Hedglen, Thomas L. "Canadian County." The Encyclopedia of Oklahoma History and Culture. www.okhistory.org.

Historic Fort Reno. "Fort Reno Historical Information." www.fortreno.org/history-2.

Hoig, Stan. "Fort Reno." The Encyclopedia of Oklahoma History and Culture. www.okhistory.org.

Killackey, Jill. "State Agency to Close Yukon Nursing Home." www.newsok.com/article/2749691/state-agency-to-close-yukon-nursing-home.

Moore, John H. "Cheyenne, Southern." The Encyclopedia of Oklahoma History and Culture. www.okhistory.org.

National Park Service. "Ben Clark." www.nps.gov/waba/learn/historyculture/ben-clark.htm.

Ross, Bobby, Jr. "Area Father Calls Lake Death Trap." www.newsok.com/article/2505359/area-father-calls-lake-death-trap.

Savage, Cynthia. "El Reno." The Encyclopedia of Oklahoma History and Culture. www.okhistory.org.

———. "Mustang." The Encyclopedia of Oklahoma History and Culture. www.okhistory.org.

———. "Piedmont." The Encyclopedia of Oklahoma History and Culture. www.okhistory.org.

———. "Union City." The Encyclopedia of Oklahoma History and Culture. www.okhistory.org.

Thiesen, Barbara A. "Every Beginning Is Hard: Darlington Mennonite Mission, 1880–1902." *Mennonite Life* 61, no. 2 (June 2006). ml.bethelks.edu/issue/vol-61-no-2/article/every-beginning-is-hard-darlington-mennonite-missi.

Washee-Freeland, Carolyn, prep. *Cheyenne and Arapaho Tribes Inventory of Significant Battles*. N.p., 2012.

Wikipedia. "Lake Overholser." en.wikipedia.org/wiki/Lake_Overholser.

Wilson, Linda D. "Arapaho." The Encyclopedia of Oklahoma History and Culture. www.okhistory.org.

About the Authors

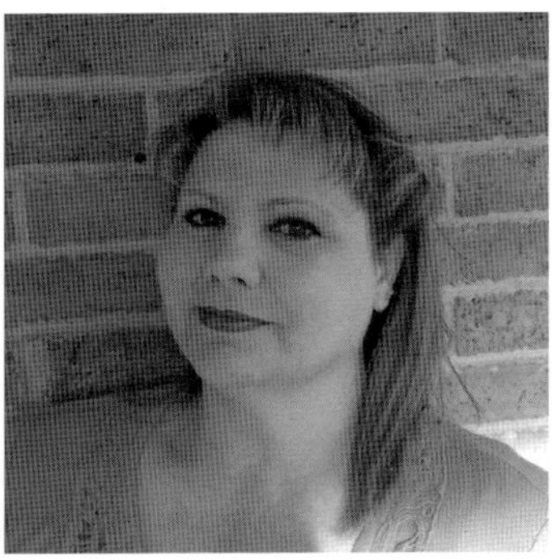

Tanya has been interested in the paranormal since the young of six, when she saw her first full-body apparition in her own home. She started researching more about the paranormal around 2001 and joined a paranormal team around 2008–09. She founded her own team in 2011, the Oklahoma Paranormal Association. As the founder of OPA and president of Paranormal Times Entertainments LLC, she is busy helping to teach others about paranormal investigating, as well as providing private investigations for the public and private home investigations for families experiencing paranormal activity in their homes or businesses. She has been featured on *My Ghost Story* as well as in many articles and newscasts. She has coauthored two books, *Haunted Guthrie* and *Haunted Oklahoma City*. Tanya has been a pediatric nurse for the past twenty years and works with special needs children. In the fall of 2018, she will teach her first paranormal class at a metro technical college, during which time she hopes to develop a special textbook to be used for future classes. She has been a speaker for paranormal events and has also organized events in Oklahoma. She is also a published children's book author, wife and mother of three. She is currently working on her next book(s) focusing on her two favorite topics, history and the paranormal, as well as a fiction mystery novel.

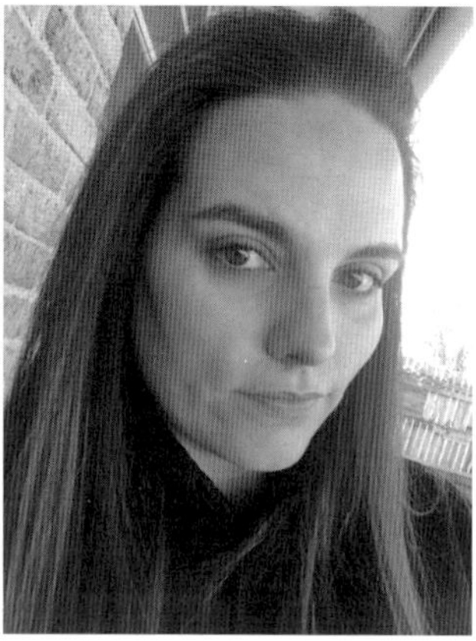

Whitney Wilson has had a long history of paranormal experiences but had never been part of a paranormal team until she joined the Oklahoma Paranormal Association in 2015. She started out as a team member and then advanced to case manager and now is the vice president of Paranormal Times Entertainments LLC/ Oklahoma Paranormal Association. Her quest for knowledge and understanding has grown. She says, "It's a great feeling to be able to back up an experience with actual history." Whitney is also a pediatric nurse, wife and mother.